SMITH & WOLLENSKY

❖ STEAK ❖

ALAN STILLMAN

PROPRIETOR

TEXT BY ESTEBAN W. DE BOURGRAVE
PHOTOGRAPHY BY BILL MILNE

FRIEDMAN/FAIRFAX
PUBLISHERS

A FRIEDMAN/FAIRFAX BOOK

© 1999 by Michael Friedman Publishing Group, Inc.

Library of Congress Cataloging-in-Publication Data available upon request

ISBN 1-56799-797-X

Photography ©1999 Bill Milne

Editor: Sharyn Rosart
Art Director: Jeff Batzli
Designer: Galen Smith
Photography Director: Christopher Bain
Production Manager: Camille Lee

Color separations by Colourscan Overseas Co. Pte. Ltd.
Printed in China by Leefung-Asco Printers Ltd.

For bulk purchases and special sales, please contact:

Friedman/Fairfax Publishers
Attention: Sales Department
15 West 26th Street
New York, NY 10010
212/685-6610 FAX 212/685-1307

Visit our website:
www.metrobooks.com

DEDICATION

& ACKNOWLEDGMENTS

To the memory of my dear mother, who served me delicious flank steak seared on the grill. I'll remember that flavor until the day that I die. And I won't forget to always slice it on the diagonal.

I'd like to thank Sharyn Rosart and Michael Friedman for giving me the chance to express myself about this, the world's most coveted food. Long may you carve!

The publishers would like to thank the staff of Smith & Wollensky and New York Restaurant Group for their assistance, particularly Tom Hart, Victor Chavez, Anne Massey, Kathleen Duffy, Daniel Thames, Patrick Colton, and Hossein Khanloo.

Over twenty-three years, we've aged well, through endeavors both rare and well-done. I thought we'd better put it all down on paper, because the guests we have served at Smith & Wollenskys across the country are the only ones who know how much fun we've been having along the way. Then again, they're in good company: twenty-three years in business and more than 10 million guests—that's a lot of fun no matter how you look at it.

So, proceed without caution. This is not a historical tribute to the grandeur of that which was, but a tip of the hat to what Smith & Wollensky is today—a great New York steakhouse that is expanding around the world. What is the recipe for a great steakhouse? Damned if I can tell you definitively, but when I walk into any one of our places on any night, and sense the rhythm of the waiters moving about, combined with the clink of silverware and wine glasses, the aroma of grilled steaks, and a steady flow of laughter and conversation from across the room, then I know all is right in the world.

Sure, we've had our fair share of major screw-ups, minor catastrophes, and general mayhem over the years. Life would be boring without them. But we've also enjoyed the glories of a two-decades-long-and-running success story, rare indeed in the high-end restaurant business. If

ABOVE: RESTAURATEUR ALAN STILLMAN ENJOYS A GLASS OF WINE WHILE WAITING FOR A PERFECTLY GRILLED STEAK.

you don't believe me, then ask the walls at Smith & Wollensky—they have ears and eyes, you know. You don't need to go to any library or archive; it's all there on the walls—great reviews and wacky photos; restaurant awards beside paintings of "award-worthy" zaftig women, letters from some of our more outspoken guests, and personal brass name plates hung over favorite tables.

The wine we've poured over the years could fill an ocean or two. From our National Wine Week celebration to the most memorable bottle from a small boutique winery, we have been able to introduce the pleasures of drinking wine with food to millions of thirsty guests. As our restaurants expand, so do our cellars, which hold one of the largest award-winning collections in the world.

I would be remiss if I didn't mention the people who make it all happen every day, 365 days a year: our managers and waitstaff. The youngest is nineteen and the oldest is eighty, with a lot of experience in

between. And they stick around for a long time, so not only do they recognize our good customers, but our regular customers come to know them even better. You can have the most magnificently designed tables and chairs, china and silver, but they are all for naught without the life and personality that is infused into a restaurant by its staff.

The late restaurateur Joe Baum often said that "people don't come to restaurants because they're hungry." I would agree. So, stay home if an empty stomach is your only concern, but come to Smith & Wollensky to have a great time. After all, it is the shared experience of being together that makes for a great meal. (Of course, a perfectly grilled steak can't hurt.)

One of our ads pictures Smith & Wollensky's exterior and boldly states: "If Steak Were a Religion, This Would Be Its Cathedral." If this were so, I think our guests gathered around a table of delicious food and wine would have to say that they're sitting in one hell of a pew.

—Alan Stillman

The Greatest Steakhouse on Earth

The word "steakhouse" brings a couple of inviting images to mind. The first is that humble place on the side of the road where you stopped to eat, back in the days when steak was a little bit pricey for your pocketbook. It was probably in the West, perhaps in the desert, and you sat at a wooden table decorated with a red-checked tablecloth and ordered your steak medium rare. The cook would do it up any way you liked, as long as you didn't ask for it well done—do that and he might chase you out the door waving his spatula. He couldn't stand ruining a good steak!

Along with your steak you had a glass of beer, or maybe some wine, and you played with a little plate of iceberg lettuce, radishes, tomatoes, and maybe an olive or two. The baked potato was pretty good, especially with sour cream and bacon bits from a jar. But you were there for the steak, a perfectly charred piece of meat that fulfilled all your desires.

These roadside steakhouses, found all over America, are usually the best restaurant for miles around, havens of rich but simple pleasures. America wouldn't be the same without these classic, homespun descendents of the cowboys' chuckwagon. Perhaps the most perfect example of this class of steakhouse was the old Bobcat Bite Cafe, which for years served steaks and hash browns and nothing else to the denizens of northern New Mexico. The customers were more than happy to postpone salad and dessert, once the cook—who was also the waiter—set their sixteen-ounce (450g) sirloin in front of them.

The second type of restaurant evoked by the word "steakhouse" is the old-world, cosmopolitan hangout found in America's great cities, like New

OPPOSITE: GOOD STEAKHOUSES OFFER A SPECIAL AMBIENCE THAT AT ONCE HEIGHTENS THE ANTICIPATION OF THE HUNGRY CUSTOMER AND SATISFIES THE COMFORTABLY REPLETE. THERE ARE SECRET CORNERS OF SMITH & WOLLENSKY THAT IMMEDIATELY TRANSPORT DINERS TO A MYTHICAL ERA WHEN THEY COULD BE CERTAIN THEIR EVERY APPETITE WOULD BE SATED.

York, Chicago, and New Orleans. In these upscale joints, the elegant, clubby atmosphere isn't diminished by fussiness, and everyone is serious about their food: they want good steak, prepared well, with knowledgeable service and a pleasant, masculine atmosphere. Steakhouses like this were everywhere at the turn of the twentieth century, but they declined, closed up, or were simply forgotten.

Fortunately, Smith & Wollensky picked up where they left off. This establishment is perhaps the culmination of this tradition, the pinnacle of the art of steak. To put it another way: Smith & Wollensky is the quintessential American steakhouse. A bite of a thick, grilled steak at Smith & Wollensky can give you the feeling that all the steak knowledge humans have accumulated over the centuries has found its way into this restaurant and onto this plate set in front of you, tempting your tastebuds. At every meal, the Smith & Wollensky restaurants in New York, Chicago, Miami, Las Vegas, and New Orleans are mobbed with people packing beefy appetites, wholeheartedly appreciating all the work that goes into making a great steak. And they usually like to accompany their meat with an equally inspired bottle of wine. It's a place to drink a lot, eat too much, and enjoy good conversation with long-lost friends or future business associates.

The New York Smith & Wollensky is located on the east side of Manhattan, not too far from the East River. Recently, a rare map dealer presented a map of Manhattan from 1820 to Smith & Wollensky founder Alan Stillman. This map showed that the current Smith & Wollensky restaurant is located right in the territory of the old Smith farmstead, where the Smith family toiled in the rocky soil bordering the East River in the late eighteenth and early nineteenth centuries.

The farm disappeared, of course, long before the United Nations and all the high-rises and town houses sprouted up in the neighborhood—before people gave up struggling with plows, horses, and manure piles, and started putting more stock in the ability to dominate a taxi driver, negotiate for opening-night theater tickets, or change the batteries in their cell phones with one hand tied behind their backs. It was, in fact, long before the current restaurant was even a twinkle in Stillman's eye—because despite its handsome old-world appearance, Smith & Wollensky was established only in 1977. Curiously, without knowing of the Smith farmstead, Stillman picked the names Smith and Wollensky at random from the New York City telephone directory.

The site Stillman chose for Smith & Wollensky was actually the location of another venerable New York culinary institution—Manny Wolf's Steakhouse, which stood on the same spot for years. (Manny Wolf's deli and caterers, a family concern, still does business nearby.)

Stillman started Smith & Wollensky, which has become an institution itself, with the idea of providing the classic New York beefsteak meal. Most of the clas-

ABOVE: AS THE SIGN SAYS, SMITH & WOLLENSKY SERVES ONLY THE BEST.

According to a survey by the National Cattlemen's Beef Association, people feel powerful when they order beef.

sic New York steakhouses of the time tended to be neglected affairs that along with their dry-aged steaks offered musty carpeting on the floors, smoke stains on the ceiling, and little in the way of elegant beverages ("You'd ask for a wine list," says Stillman, "and the waiter would say, 'Whadayamean a list—ya want red or white?'"). So Stillman designed a beautiful interior with wood paneling, skylights, wainscoted banquettes, marble stairs, smoky mirrors, and a clean wooden floor. Oh, and there's also the painting of a nude woman reclining on a lily pad. No one knows why it is there.

Over the years, Stillman's eclectic art collection has established itself on every surface, with fetching nudes growing the walls, including a seven-foot-tall

(2.1m) beauty shyly covering her privates on the stairway, as the stuffed head of a seventeen-point elk stares lasciviously at her from across the way. And there's a Holstein-Friesian bull nearby, just in case you forget why you're there.

While the art collection has evolved over time, the menu has stayed pretty much the same: gigantic dry-aged steaks, chops and racks of lamb, and over-sized portions of seafood, accompanied by such classic steakhouse fare as creamed spinach, asparagus, and absurdly delicious hash-brown potatoes. Typically, most of the tables, even at lunch, are well supplied with wine, followed by cognac or jumbo snifters of other digestifs.

OPPOSITE: MANNY WOLF'S RESTAURANT AT THE CORNER OF 49TH STREET AND THIRD AVENUE. **ABOVE**: PROPRIETOR ALAN STILLMAN HAS A PASSION NOT ONLY FOR DELICIOUS STEAK, BUT ALSO FOR ART, AS EVIDENCED BY THIS RUBENESQUE NUDE HANGING PROUDLY ON THE WALL AT SMITH & WOLLENSKY'S HOME BASE IN NEW YORK.

Beef is eaten almost eighty million times a day in the United States.

OPPOSITE: EACH OF THE SMITH & WOLLENSKY RESTAURANTS HAS THOUSANDS OF BOTTLES OF WINES ON HAND—ENOUGH TO SATISFY ANY OENOPHILIC DESIRE. THESE WOODEN SHELVES FILL THE GRAND WINE CELLAR IN THE NEW YORK RESTAURANT. **BELOW**: ALAN STILLMAN VIEWS WINE AS A THING OF BEAUTY, AND THAT VISION INCLUDES THE BOTTLES.

The wine business is very serious. Stillman is well known for picking future winners, and some of the bottles he bought in the past for about one hundred dollars, such as an '89 Pétrus, an '85 Lafite-Rothschild, and an '87 Opus One, are now worth well over a thousand dollars apiece. In fact, he's done so well that not long ago he had to thin out his stock by selling a few cases through Christie's auction house. Many of Smith & Wollensky's customers take wine just as seriously as Stillman does. It is not unusual for someone to scan the 350-entry wine list and plop down more than three hundred dollars for something like an '84 Jordan Cabernet. Most of the wines are red, and most of them are hearty enough to not be overwhelmed by a fine piece of steak. The most popular wine at Smith & Wollensky in New York is Robert Mondavi Cabernet Sauvignon—in fact, that restaurant is the biggest seller of Robert Mondavi wine in the world.

Few customers see the wine cellar, but those who do are amazed. All told, the Smith & Wollensky restaurants in New York, Miami, Chicago, New Orleans, and Las Vegas have about a quarter of a million bottles on hand at any given time. In the New York restaurant, a vast room of wooden racks holds about fifty thousand bottles. The tops of wine crates decorating the racks tell the story of this wine cellar: Premier Grand Cru Château Haut Brion '64; Grand Vin de Lafite-Rothschild '66; Château Margaux Grand Vin '83; Lynch Bages Pauillac '86.

Fine wine has helped Smith & Wollensky to be successful since its inception. Typically, the Manhattan branch serves up to sixteen hundred steak meals a day. Thanks to the brilliant layout, however, each customer feels like they are in a well-attended clubroom, surrounded by like-minded carnivores who enjoy a good glass of red wine with their meat. Everything is peaceful in the dining room. The waiters, who hail from Yugoslavia, Spain, Chile, the United States, and other locales, and all seem to have worked at the restaurant for ages, move carefully about, tending to everyone's needs. The only customers privy to the real behind-the-scenes work are those lucky seven or eight sitting at the round table in the semi-private alcove with floor-to-ceiling windows that look directly into the kitchen, not a chop's throw from the cooks. From this table, they get a clear view of the action.

ABOVE: NOTHING COMPLEMENTS A GOOD STEAK LIKE A FULL-BODIED RED.

OPPOSITE: CRATE-ENDS FROM SOME OF THE SOMMELIER'S FAVORITE SELECTIONS ARE TACKED ONTO THE WINE-CELLAR RACKS.

OPPOSITE: A RARE MOMENT OF DOWNTIME FINDS A CHEF'S TOQUE RESTING NEXT TO A SHARP KNIFE ON TOP OF THE KITCHEN LINE. ONCE THE DOORS OPEN, THOSE PLATES WILL FLY OFF THE COUNTER.

The leanest steaks come from the loin and the round. Eye round and top round steaks have only four grams of fat per three-ounce (85g) cooked serving.

They see longtime chef Victor Chavez standing in his toque directing traffic, as the cooks behind the stainless steel line prepare perfect steaks, chops, and other dishes in a syncopated dance that illustrates the chaos theory. How can they possibly produce so many wonderful meals at such a rapid clip? The secret lies in great planning and lots of preparation.

Before daylight, the head buyer pulls open the service door at the 49th Street entrance of the Smith & Wollensky building and begins the hours of inventory and ordering that lead up to lunch. The restaurant is hushed at this time of day, and he makes his way quietly up and down the three flights of stairs that connect the various kitchens. He checks the aging room to see how the endless wooden racks of steaks are getting along. (Fine, thank you.) And he makes sure there are enough vegetables, potatoes (more than a thousand pounds [454kg] of hand-peeled spuds a day), and other delights to keep the place in tune.

Soon the cooks and butchers arrive to prepare for lunch. Pastry chef Hossein Khanloo sequesters himself in a windowless room, armed with a rolling pin and plenty of fresh butter and other rich ingredients, to produce the timeless desserts that people somehow find room for after demolishing their steaks. He makes carrot cake (requiring fifty pounds [22.7kg] of carrots a week), pecan pie (with forty pounds [18.1kg] of pecans and ten gallons of bourbon sauce, at least, each week—enough for more than six hundred slices), and other favorites fresh each morning. Meanwhile, in the butchering area, a team of pros has pulled thirty-five or so well-aged rib sections from the meat lockers, to be trimmed and cut into steaks for the day's run. And that's only the beginning. For several hours the butchering room is a frenzy of curved knives, band saws, and friendly banter as the butchers trim out the following meat to send upstairs to the kitchens:

300 SIRLOIN STEAKS

5 DOUBLE SIRLOINS, BIG ENOUGH FOR TWO PEOPLE

500 FILETS MIGNONS

7 CHÂTEAUBRIANDS, BIG ENOUGH FOR TWO PEOPLE

100 RIB STEAKS

8 FULL PRIME RIBS

45 PORTIONS OF RACK OF LAMB

40 JUMBO VEAL CHOPS

PAGE 20: ALL SMITH & WOLLENSKY STEAKS ARE DRY-AGED IN SPACIOUS WALK-IN COOLERS. THIS OLD-WORLD METHOD TAKES WEEKS BUT THE END RESULT—PLATTERS OF THE FINEST BEEF—IS WORTH THE EFFORT. PAGE 21: FLAME-BROILED IS MORE THAN JUST A PHRASE AT SMITH & WOLLENSKY. THE CHEFS LOVE THE HEAT IN THE KITCHEN, BECAUSE IT COOKS STEAKS BEST. BELOW: IT'S TIME TO EAT BEEF. OPPOSITE: YOU DON'T HAVE TO BE FAMOUS TO GET YOUR NAME ENGRAVED ON A BRASS PLAQUE AND AFFIXED TO THE CHAIR RAIL. YOU SIMPLY MUST BE A GOOD AND HAPPY CUSTOMER.

Once that's done, the butchers pull out a hundred or so Cajun rib steaks, which have been marinating in a potent mixture of garlic, onions, hot pepper, and other spices for two days, and dry them off for the lunch and dinner trade. They then cut about a hundred more of the ribs to put in a fresh marinade for future use. And a few dozen chicken breasts are prepped, along with swordfish, lump crab, and lobsters. All the while, hits from the 1960s come softly over the speakers, so that veal chops are trimmed by happy butchers singing along to "Jimmy Mack" and "Stop (In the Name of Love)."

Down the hall and around the corner, still more cooks carefully assemble the creamed spinach (fifteen bushels of spinach a day), hash browns, salads, and other soul-satisfying side dishes. A woman washes the linens (four thousand napkins a day). Everywhere, delivery men and some of the thirty cooks and three sous chefs are attending to myriad tasks and running up and down the "secret" stairs that connect the three floors of kitchens serving the restaurant.

It is a major production for a big restaurant that cares about its customers and knows what they want: "You come here to eat big portions of the very best meat, eat well, and leave full," says Chef Chavez.

At about ten o'clock the waiters and waitresses appear and start setting up the dining room, speaking in several languages. They polish the crystal, set out the tablecloths, and make sure the place looks presentable for the regulars who will start drifting in around noon. When they are finished, they listen to a pep talk from their supervisor, and then stand in wait for customer number one. Meanwhile, in back, Chef Chavez adjusts his toque, rolls up his sleeves, and the service begins. There are no heat lamps in the Smith & Wollensky kitchen because everything is cooked fast and goes out fast.

While the kitchen operates in a state of controlled chaos, out front the dining rooms are calm, filled with business people, tourists, the idle rich, and the simply carnivorous, contentedly waiting for what they know will be superb examples of the steak arts. Is that Mayor Rudy Giuliani sitting over there? Such a sight wouldn't be surprising. Lots of famous people come to the restaurant, and you'll find their names etched on small brass plaques affixed to chair rails along most of the restaurant's walls. But the curious thing is, you have to be much more than a celebrity to see your name there. You have to be a regular customer. And you have to be a steak lover. And if he fulfills that description, Joe Schmo is just as likely as the biggest star in Hollywood to get a plaque in his name. Because Smith & Wollensky is about steaks, and nothing but steaks.

OPPOSITE: Smith & Wollensky waiters have been around long enough to know what customers like—brisk, efficient service, with a kind nod if not a full smile, and a nice selection of bread with their meals. Here, a waiter organizes a tray in the New York kitchen.

The fastest-cooking steak is the thin-cut round tip, which is used for steak sandwiches. At about one-eighth to one-quarter inch (3 to 6mm) thick, it cooks in just one to two minutes.

BEEFSTEAK DINNER

◆

"The New York steak dinner, or 'beefsteak,' is a form of gluttony as stylized and regional as the riverbank fish fry, the hot-rock clambake, or the Texas barbecue," wrote Joseph Mitchell in his *New Yorker* essay "All You Can Hold for Five Bucks." While Smith & Wollensky grew out of the more refined tradition of gaslight steakhouses serving beautiful cuts of meat, it owes a lot to messy beefsteak dinners, too. There is no denying that the early twentieth-century "beefsteaks" contributed greatly to New York's reputation as a place where people were awfully serious about steak.

Hosted by politicians, clubs, and anyone with something big to celebrate, these "beefsteaks" were usually held in large social halls, cellars, saloons, and

OPPOSITE: THIS ENTICING STILL LIFE OF WINE AND BEEF IS TYPICAL OF THE SMITH & WOLLENSKY TABLE WHEREVER IT IS FOUND. ABOVE: YOU DON'T NEED SHARP KNIVES FOR SMITH & WOLLENSKY STEAKS, BUT THEY SUPPLY THEM ANYWAY.

Steakhouses have about 75 percent more customers today than they did in 1993.

BELOW: THE KEY TO GOOD EATING IS GREAT MARBLING, PERFECT DRY AGING, AND QUALITY CONTROL. EVERY CUT OF BEEF IS TAGGED THE MOMENT IT ENTERS THE RESTAURANTS, SO ITS PROGRESS TO PERFECTION CAN BE MONITORED. **OPPOSITE**: NEW YORK SMITH & WOLLENSKY CHEF VICTOR CHAVEZ REMOVES A PERFECTLY COOKED STEAK FROM THE FIRE.

even bowling alleys. They were strictly stag affairs until women got the right to vote—and thus became valuable to politicians courting votes at beefsteaks. But their underlying structure remained almost comically masculine and pared to the bone.

According to Mitchell, the patrons sat around big tables, wearing aprons to wipe their hands with, and big paper chef's hats emblazoned with slogans such as "It's hell when your wife is a widow." No napkins or utensils were allowed, and if you didn't feel like eating with your hands, well then, you were going to go hungry.

The saturnalia began with appetizers such as grilled miniature beef burgers on onion slices, crab cocktails, olives, and crudités, followed by sliced steak served on day-old bread or fresh toast (much like the steak Smith & Wollensky serves today). Pitchers of beer linked one course to the next.

Each guest was expected to eat five or six small servings of this sliced steak before the waiters appeared with more beer and platters of double-wide lamb chops, which they set down in the middle of the table. Everyone grabbed one or two chops with their greasy fingers and chomped them down, all the while hoping for more, and following every couple of bites with a slug of beer. By this time, the crowd was generally raucous, greasy, and otherwise well-lubricated, and the hall was filled with the din of bad jokes and noisemakers and a band playing stalwarts like "Ol' Man River." Perhaps a politician or two would try to make a speech, but the serious work continued at tableside as the waiters brought out platters of grilled lamb kidneys. "I'm so full I'm about to pop," Mitchell quotes one man as saying. "Push those kidneys a little closer if you don't mind."

Those who weren't too drunk to chew, or too full to wave to the waiter, would insist that the chefs keep the grills fired up and the steaks coming. "If you're able to hold a little more when you start home, you haven't been to a beefsteak, you've been to a banquet that they called a beefsteak," wrote Mitchell.

STEAK CONSUMPTION UP

Steak keeps gaining in popularity, year after year. In 1997, more than 364 million steaks were served in U.S. restaurants, an increase of 4 percent over 1996. A total of 6.9 billion servings of beef are served annually

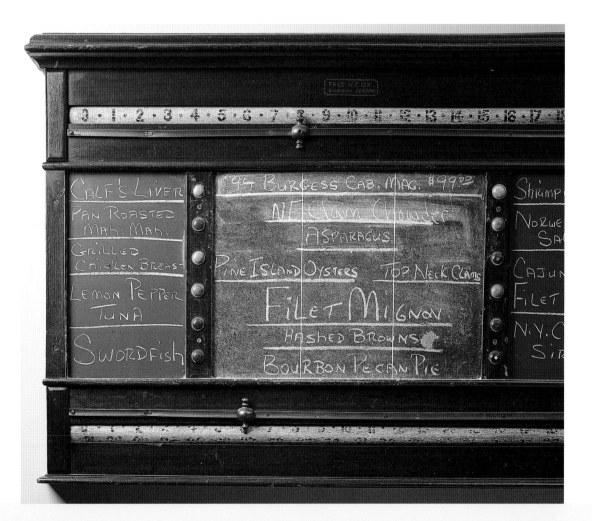

OPPOSITE: IN THE QUIET BEFORE THE STORM, CORNER TABLES WAIT FOR ANXIOUS CUSTOMERS WHO WILL QUICKLY BE LULLED INTO SOMNOLENCE BY GRAND PORTIONS OF STEAK AND WINE. **ABOVE:** THE SPECIALS CHANGE DAILY—SOMETIMES HOURLY—SO BE SURE TO CHECK THE CHALKBOARDS.

in U.S. restaurants, compared with 4.2 billion servings of poultry, 1.8 billion of fish and other seafood, and 300 million of pork.

Steak is still the most coveted form of beef. That could be because busy North Americans, with less and less time to cook elaborate meals, are sticking to one-dish dinners at home. While beef is still the most favored source of protein at dinner tables in the United States and Canada alike, the old-style meat-and-potatoes dinner is starting to fall by the wayside as people become more health-conscious. This might be part of the reason people take such pleasure in ordering a thick, juicy steak at a restaurant. More than ever, a perfect steak is a special treat.

STEAKS PER STEER

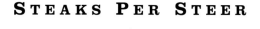

When you look at a steer, you might see a walking, mooing steak factory, but the fact is, steaks are only a small part of the animal. That's why steak is such a treat—in addition to tasting great when served rare, it is rare. According to the American Meat Institute, the average steer, which might weigh upwards of twelve hundred pounds (540kg) before slaughter, yields only about fifty-eight pounds (26.3kg) of rib and loin steaks. That's about 20 percent of the entire animal. No wonder T-bones cost so much: there are only about ten pounds (4.5kg) of them on each steer.

If you multiply the number of steers brought to market each month by the number of steaks on each animal, it averages out to only one steak per American per month. Be sure to get your share.

EARLY MEAT-EATERS

There is a popular notion that early humans—the people we imagine lived in caves, wore animal skins, and dragged each other around by the hair—were great steak-eaters. We picture them sitting around the fire gnawing on a good-sized bone. Many people would admit to feeling a little cave-dweller excitement when a gigantic Smith & Wollensky bone-in rib steak is set in front of them. Another thought that comes to mind is: Fred Flintstone would have loved this. But in fact, the cave folk probably never saw a two-pound (1kg) rib steak.

Science has largely put the idea of cave people gorging on red meat to rest. Judging by the patterns of wear and tear on fossilized teeth, protohumans ate a lot more fruit than meat. And in the Book of Genesis, God gives Adam and Eve a lot of plants to eat, but doesn't mention where their meat will come from.

Early humans were hunter-gatherers, and as you can imagine, it was a lot easier to grab a few pieces of fruit off a tree than to chase down an antelope, kill it with bare hands, skin it with a sharp

BELOW: Tough wooden menu boards hark back to the grand steakhouse days of old New York.

C A J U N   F I L E T   M I G N O N

SERVES: 4

PREPARATION TIME: 20 minutes, plus marinating time

INGREDIENTS

For the Cajun spice rub:

1 TEASPOON CAYENNE PEPPER

1 TEASPOON GROUND BLACK PEPPER

1 TEASPOON GROUND WHITE PEPPER

1 TEASPOON CHILI POWDER

1 TEASPOON HACOMAT SEASONING

1 TEASPOON PAPRIKA

1 TEASPOON GARLIC POWDER

1 TEASPOON THYME

1 TEASPOON BASIL

1 TEASPOON OREGANO

1/2 TEASPOON CUMIN

4 6-OUNCE PIECES FILET MIGNON

1 SMALL ONION, MINCED

VEGETABLE OIL TO COVER THE STEAKS

BOTTLED AU POIVRE SAUCE TO TASTE

INSTRUCTIONS

Combine all the spices and rub the mixture into the steaks. Lightly perforate the steaks with a fork so the seasoning penetrates into the meat. Place the meat in a small, deep pan. Add the onion and enough oil to cover the meat. Marinate in the refrigerator for 1 to 2 hours. When ready to cook, remove the meat from the marinade. Sear the steaks at high heat for about one minute on each side, then continue cooking over lower heat to desired doneness. Serve each steak on a pool of au poivre sauce and garnish with steamed vegetables, if desired.

rock, then roast it on some sticks. Just maybe not as satisfying.

About ten thousand years ago a neolithic hunter-gatherer somehow persuaded a few animals to stay around the caveyard, and, voilà, livestock was born. Since agricultural science was developing around this time, there were grain and leftover plants to feed the animals. Eating meat suddenly became easier. Humans were able to choose what they planted and raised, rather than wandering the land looking for good grub among the plants and animals that nature offered. So they chose meat. Cattle were domesticated in the Middle East about 6500 B.C.

In ancient times, poor people probably ate a lot of grain and only a little meat, while rich people feasted on steak—not that different from today, really. The heroes of the *Odyssey* ate a lot of barbecued meat, and the Romans were famous for gorging on roasts. In the Middle Ages the trend continued, with peasants eating whatever they could grow, and the wealthy flavoring their beef roasts by stuffing partridges inside of pigs inside of cows. By the 1700s, the average European got about 10 to 25 percent of his or her calories from meat; North Americans ate much more, due to the great quantities of wild game in the colonies. Then, with the growth of cowboying and cattle ranching, beef entered the North American diet in a big way. It wasn't long before beef was king, and our diet was forever changed. Steakhouses weren't far behind.

AMERICAN BEEF

No one knows exactly when the first head of cattle tasted American range grass, but we can be certain that the animal was happy to be here. Aside from Argentina, with its wonderful pampas, no place else offered rangeland like North America. Revisionist historians would bet good money that the Vikings were the first to bring cattle to North America, but it is less controversial to assume that the first cattle arrived sometime after Columbus dropped anchor in Hispaniola with his *bisték*-loving crew. He had cattle with him on his second voyage in 1493, and it is likely that some survived to produce offspring in Santo Domingo.

In the early fifteenth century, Cortés brought Spanish cattle, the precursors of the Texas Longhorn, to Mexico. A few decades later, the explorer Coronado brought cattle with him to keep his strength up while he searched for the fabled city of gold. Unfortunately, Las Vegas didn't exist then, and the expedition was a failure. But the cattle thrived, thanks no doubt to their half-wild nature, descended as they were from the cattle depicted in cave drawings on the Iberian Peninsula.

By the early seventeenth century there was a network of Spanish forts and ranches all across what is now the border area of Mexico and the United States. Some of these cattle escaped and eventually became

the storied Texas Longhorn breed, the foundation of the modern cattle industry. It is a good thing that the breed continued to evolve, with new gene lines imported from Europe and elsewhere—apparently, the meat on those early Texas Longhorns was rather tough.

The Longhorns, which were gradually bred to greater tenderness, made up the first huge cattle drives from San Antonio to French Louisiana in the early eighteenth century. They weren't intended so much for food as for hides and fat, and many were used to pull

wagons back west, labor that was far more valuable to the early settlers than a big steak. In the 1780s, about fifteen thousand cattle a year were driven east across Texas toward New Orleans; these smaller cattle drives continued into the nineteenth century. By 1840, the Shawnee Trail followed a well-established route from Texas up through Kansas City to Sedalia, Missouri, and St. Louis. The cattle drivers had to contend with Comanche warriors, Kansas bushwhackers, rustlers, and all manner of natural troublemakers, such as

rattlesnakes, tornados, and dust devils. This trail shifted westward at the beginning of the Civil War, leaving Abilene and heading toward western Kansas and Colorado to meet the trains.

But it wasn't until the Civil War ended that the legendary cattle drives of Hollywood movies came into being. Between 1865 and 1895, more than ten million cattle trudged the dusty trails between Texas and the railhead cities in the northern states of Colorado, Kansas, and Missouri. Because they arrived stringy and tired from the long trail, the cattle were often fattened up at the end of the trail on the wild grasslands before being shipped east and west by rail. Most of the trails started in the San Antonio area, and without

OPPOSITE: A CRACKLIN' PORTION OF MEATY PORK SHANK WILL SATISFY ANY APPETITE.

ABOVE: COWBOYS ON A CATTLE DRIVE BREAK FOR A MIDDAY MEAL.

ABOVE: A STOCKYARD IN KANSAS CITY, WHERE TEXAS LONGHORNS WERE FATTENED UP AFTER THEY ARRIVED TOUGH AND STRINGY FROM THE TRAIL.

Nobody seems to know which Diane the dish refers to, but Steak Diane was invented at the swinging Copacabana Palace Hotel in Rio de Janeiro. The chef there pounded steaks until they were thin, sautéed them in butter, flamed them with cognac, and then added sherry, butter, and chives.

these cattle drives, it is doubtful that Austin, Houston, Waco, Fort Worth, Dallas, Tulsa, Dodge City, Abilene, or Kansas City would be anywhere near as prosperous as they are today.

It was during these epic drives that the chuckwagon came into being. (Cattleman Charles Goodnight is credited with inventing this contraption in 1866.) There were a lot of people to feed on a cattle drive, and not much time to do it in. Then as now, time was money. So the crews always hired a cook, usually calling him "Cookie"—the name given to Gabby Hayes in so many Hollywood Westerns—and outfitted him with a chuckwagon. This very sturdy wagon would be carefully stocked with enough chow to last the four or five months a cattle drive could be expected to take.

Food was important to the cowboys, so the cook had the power to set and enforce a wide range of rules to insure that the cattle drive would be well run. For instance, no one was allowed to gallop into camp—unlike in the movies—because the dust clouds could ruin good beef, beans, and biscuits (about all there ever was to eat). Cranky, cantankerous, downright ornery—these were the words used to describe Cookie. And you would be a bit irritable, too, if you had to cook over prairie coal: dried buffalo chips and cow pies.

The cattle drives continued on into the twentieth century, but improved transportation soon made walking cattle from state to state unnecessary.

Meanwhile, starting in the late nineteenth century, breeders began to cross English cattle with the Longhorns. Subsequently, Shorthorns, Herefords, and Angus cattle began to take over the genetic lines from the Longhorns, resulting in fatter, beefier, and more productive strains of cattle. Then, in the 1960s, breeders started looking to European breeds that were known for getting fattened up to market weight much faster, and therefore didn't require as much grain. The Limousin and the Charolais from France, and the Chianina from Italy were all brought over and are now an established part of the American cattle bloodline.

BRANDING CATTLE

Brands were used long before cowboys appeared in the North American West. The ancient Egyptians were known to have marked their cattle with designs. Cortés etched crosses into the herd he maintained in Central America as he overpowered the Aztecs. The surviving natives picked up on this and eventually taught it to the American *vaqueros*, or cowboys. While these days most cattle aren't branded, some are still marked with brands registered with the local government to prevent confusion, and to ensure that when cattle rustlers are caught, the stolen cattle can be returned to the rightful owner. The term "maverick" is

OPPOSITE: THEY STAR IN THE RESTAURANT'S ADVERTISEMENTS. THEY MAKE THE CUSTOMERS HAPPY. SMITH & WOLLENSKY'S SERVICE STAFF KNOW ALL ABOUT STEAK, APPRECIATE FINE WINE, AND THEY EVEN SEEM TO ENJOY THEIR WORK—MANY HAVE BEEN WITH THE RESTAURANT SINCE DAY ONE.

from the name of Sam Maverick (1803–1870), who didn't believe in branding. He must not have lasted long in the cattle business!

LOST LONGHORNS

The breeding of beefier, more tender cattle that could be contained in stockyards was very nearly the demise of the Texas Longhorn of song and screen. Their meat was just too stringy to make them worthwhile once cattle were being transported by train from Texas, and no longer had to walk halfway across the country. In the 1860s there were perhaps forty million Longhorns in the Texas area. By 1927, the federal government was compelled to earmark three thousand dollars to try to reestablish the nearly lost breed in the United States, according to Merle Ellis, author of *The Great American Meat Book*.

A gentleman named Will. C. Barnes covered nearly five thousand miles (8,000km) of southern Texas and northern Mexico ranchland before he found twenty cows, four calves, and three bulls to start a new herd of Longhorns. That effort paid off, but slowly. In 1960

there were twenty-five hundred Longhorns in Texas, and now there are more than forty thousand.

Curiously, the Longhorn is now considered a possible savior in developing countries, because it can range across dry, dusty land, eating scrub brush, poor quality grasses, and even cactus. That's an advantage in countries whose people cannot afford to fatten cattle on grain. And the Longhorns do not lose many calves at birth, unlike some other breeds. Ellis predicts that with all the research and crossbreeding being done on Longhorns, the steer of the future might be a large, beefy animal that likes eating on the open range and proudly wears a pair of long horns—and yields more and larger steaks.

DNA

In the United States and other countries where cattle can be grain fed, wranglers might very soon have to learn to read DNA as well as rope and ride. Since tough steaks are shunned by every steak lover, the cattle industry is trying constantly to find ways to ensure that every steak in the market is tender and juicy, even before it is aged. Now geneticists are looking at cattle with an eye toward breeding those that have the most tender cuts of meat. Scientists will examine the tenderness, marbling, size, carcass weight, and yield of more than seven thousand head of cattle. Then they'll look for gene markers, to see if any of these desirable qualities are in the genes, and therefore can be passed on to calves. Sixteen different cattle marketing associations are participating in this study, because, in the future, one association might want to concentrate on the marbling in the beef produced by a certain breed, while another might want to boost a particular breed's tenderness. Then those breeds might be crossed to make an animal that can produce an even better-tasting steak.

The genetic test being developed will help ranchers predict what a certain head of cattle will be worth almost from the day it is born. The test will also allow a rancher to check a calf for gene markers indicating whether that calf will grow up tender, or produce big steaks, or just be well marbled. Today a rancher has to wait several years, until the calf grows up and goes to market, to find the answers to these questions.

WOMEN AND CATTLE

Traditionally, steak-eating has been considered a "masculine" pursuit that sometimes seemed to preclude the participation of women. A group of guys get together and what do they eat? Salads? Not usually. Steaks. Potatoes. Brews. Maybe followed by a satisfied grunt—that's the cliché, anyway. It can all be traced back to the cattle drives, led by rangy cowpokes in leather chaps who sat around the fire at night belching, eating beans, and slicing pieces of rare steak off the spit. Steak was supposedly reserved as a rite of fellowhood among working men.

In truth, women played an important role in the growth of the cattle industry in the United States, and our nation's subsequent obsession with steaks, according to the comprehensive book *Women of the Range: Women's Roles in the Texas Beef Cattle Industry*, by Elizabeth Maret.

That role began in the earliest days of the territory we now call Texas, when King Charles II of Spain sent sixteen Spanish families to run ranches across the rough land. Three of the families were soon headed by women, including one Doña Rosa

OPPOSITE: A STEAK IS BEST EATEN UNADORNED, ESPECIALLY IF IT'S DRY-AGED AND PERFECTLY COOKED, LIKE THIS SIRLOIN. BUT THAT DOESN'T MEAN YOU SHOULDN'T CLEAR THE PALATE WITH A SIP OF GOOD WINE BETWEEN BITES.

CREAMED SPINACH

SERVES: 8

PREPARATION TIME: 50 minutes

INGREDIENTS

5 LBS. FRESH CUT SPINACH, WASHED

1 STICK BUTTER

2 OZ. SHALLOTS, DICED

1 QUART (4 CUPS) MILK

3/4 CUP FLOUR

SALT AND PEPPER TO TASTE

INSTRUCTIONS

Cook spinach in a large pot in plenty of boiling water for 10 minutes. Drain and let cool. Chop the spinach and place it in a bowl. For the béchamel sauce, melt the butter in a saucepan and sauté the shallots in the butter until translucent. In a separate pan, heat the milk just until small bubbles form on the edges of the pan. Add the flour to the butter and stir until the mixture is uniform. Add to the hot milk, stir to dissolve any lumps, and simmer for 30 to 40 minutes. Stir the béchamel sauce into the chopped spinach, season to taste, and serve.

BELOW: VELVETY CREAMED SPINACH IS A FAVORITE ACCOMPANIMENT
FOR SMITH & WOLLENSKY STEAKS—THE NEW YORK RESTAURANT GOES THROUGH
FIFTEEN BUSHELS OF SPINACH EVERY DAY.

Hinojosa de Balli, who controlled fifty-three thousand acres (21,200ha) in the Rio Grande Valley. At the beginning of the nineteenth century there were thirty cattle ranches in Texas, five of them controlled by women. And in the twentieth century, Henrietta Chamberlain King built the King Ranch, which she had founded with her husband, into one of the largest cattle enterprises ever, with more than a million acres (400,000ha) and almost a hundred thousand head of cattle. The King Ranch even developed its own strain of cattle, called San Gertrudis, which was the first new breed developed in North America. You can bet Mrs. King spent more time eating steak than cooking it!

PAGE 48: SIZZLING STEAKS FRESH FROM THE BROILER AND READY TO BE PLATED. **PAGE 49:** THE VEAL CHOP IS A WONDROUS CUT; THE AROMA ALONE MAKES THE MOUTH WATER. **BELOW:** YOU SAY YOU'LL ONLY TAKE ONE BITE, BUT CARROT CAKE NEVER RESTS LONG ON THE PLATE.

UNCLE SAM

❖

Uncle Sam was a steak man, according to Merle Ellis in *The Great American Meat Book.* Apparently, a Troy, New York, meat packer by the name of Samuel Wilson supplied meat to soldiers who were training near his plant for the War of 1812. Wilson's buddies affectionately called him "Uncle Sam" long before there was any legendary character of that name. As it happened, he stamped "US" on each barrel of meat he delivered to the army base, because it was for the federal government. The soldiers, knowing where the beef came from, started calling it "Uncle Sam's beef." The term started to spread across the country as the

Troy soldiers were transferred to different bases, and wherever the soldiers would see federal property stamped US, they called it "Uncle Sam's." Cartoonists caught on, and by the time Wilson died, in 1854, Uncle Sam was the cartoon personification of our government. Ellis says Thomas Nast was the cartoonist who thought up the pointed beard, vest, wild pants, and star-studded top hat. Finally, in 1961, the U.S. Congress passed a resolution giving credit where credit was due: Samuel Wilson, the butcher from Troy, was officially designated the basis for Uncle Sam.

CANADIAN STEAKS

Beef is pretty much as popular in Canada as it is in the United States, and vast ranches are spread across the country's central and western provinces. Canadian beef buyers, however, have recently received a little extra assistance in the form of more informative labels. In the past, apparently, some Canadians found meat labeling inadequate, because the anatomical names given to most cuts of beef didn't give a clue as to how they should be cooked. That led to improperly prepared beef, and dissatisfied eaters. It also meant that most consumers just bought the cuts they were familiar with, and prepared the same steaks over and over. In a consumer survey, one in three Canadians reported they would not buy a cut of meat that they didn't already know how to prepare. In an attempt to help people choose the best cut for their dinner, the Canadian Beef Information Center devised a new labeling system for beef, which includes the cooking method along with the name of the cut. This means a strip loin steak is now called a strip loin grilling steak, and a blade steak is a blade simmering steak. Even though the change is purely voluntary, about 75 percent of beef sold in Canada features the new labels. The idea has boosted beef sales dramatically.

Similar confusion exists in U.S. markets, with younger shoppers in particular unable to tell the difference between a sirloin steak and a T-bone. In an attempt to remedy this lack of beef knowledge, the National Cattlemen's Beef Association has started developing ways to inform consumers, including labels that provide cooking instructions for the various cuts along with the price, for those who like to know better what they are paying for.

AMERICAN BEEF ABROAD

In a typical year the United States exports more than two billion tons (1.8 billion t) of beef to countries including Japan, Mexico, Canada, Korea, and Russia. People in Asia and the Pacific Rim buy 80 percent of all U.S. beef exports. Japan buys more than any other country.

The favorite cuts in Japan are boneless ribs, brisket, and loin, according to the U.S. Department of Agriculture and the National Cattlemen's Beef Association. They prefer to eat beef at home rather than in restaurants, preparing it as steaks, and in curries and sukiyakis. An interesting way the Japanese serve steak is sliced raw into thin slices and presented on a platter near a pot of boiling broth. Each person dips an individual portion of beef in the broth to cook it, much like fondue.

South Koreans prefer to eat beef in restaurants. One favorite is Korean barbecue, with diners cooking their own beef on a grill set into the restaurant table. Steak cuts are very popular, especially in the four- and five-star restaurants.

Mexicans often eat U.S. beef in upscale hotel restaurants. Steaks are king, and rib eye, sirloin, and skirt steaks top the list. Mexicans often eat the steaks American-style, or sliced and served with hot chiles and tortillas, or in casseroles.

Loin and rib steaks are gaining in popularity in Taiwan, although they are still considered a rare luxury. As the Taiwanese learn to appreciate beef, they are turning more and more to steaks served in nice restaurants, and the island is considered a growth market for U.S. beef exports.

MARK TWAIN'S HEAVENLY BEEF

◆

Mark Twain returned from a trip to Europe with the following thoughts about Continental steaks:

Imagine a poor exile contemplating that inert thing and imagine an angel suddenly sweeping down out of a better land and setting before him a mighty porter-house steak an inch and a half [4cm] thick, hot and sputtering from the griddle; dusted with fragrant pepper; enriched with little melting bits of butter of the most unimpeachable freshness and genuineness; the precious juices of the meat trickling out and joining the gravy, archipelagoed with mushrooms; a township or two of tender, yellowish fat gracing an outlying district of the ample country of beefsteak; the long white bone which divides the sirloin from the tenderloin still in its place; and imagine that the angel also adds a great cup of American home-made coffee, with the cream a-froth on the top, some real butter, firm and yellow and fresh, some smoking hot biscuits, a plate of hot buckwheat cakes, with transparent syrup—could words describe the gratitude of this exile?

ABOVE: OPEN LATE, AND ALWAYS ELEGANTLY CASUAL, WOLLENSKY'S GRILL SERVES CUSTOMERS LOOKING FOR

A QUICK BITE, BUT EVERY MORSEL IS JUST AS DELICIOUS AS WHAT THEY'D FIND IN THE MAIN DINING ROOMS.

PAMPAS GAUCHOS AND THEIR GREAT STEAKS

Walk down the streets of any Argentine town in the early afternoon and the air is fragrant with the smell of grilling steaks. Argentinians take their beef seriously, and have done so since the eighteenth century, when the legendary gauchos first began raising cattle on the pampas. While gaucho culture, like American cowboy culture, is now as much myth as reality, the Argentinian love of beef is solid fact.

While modern Argentinians no longer stuff themselves with two hundred pounds (90.8kg) of beef per man, woman, and child each year, as they did in the 1960s, they still consume about half a pound (227g) per day per person. That puts them in the top rank of the world's beef eaters, followed by their neighbors in Uruguay.

The gauchos liked to roast beef on open fires, and used their intimidating knives to slice off steaks. It is said that they ate little else, a predilection that prompted Charles Darwin to complain that he couldn't find a decent vegetable or piece of fruit in the entire country. It is still difficult to find a salad more complex than sliced tomatoes and onions, perhaps topped with cheese and boiled eggs, in any of Argentina's many *parillas* and *churrascarias* (steak joints). This food is not light: a typical Argentinian side dish is a plate of blood sausage (sometimes sweetened with orange and walnuts), tripe, ribs, and kidneys. Another option is French fries doused with garlic and parsley sauce. And there is always a dish of *chimichurri*, an Argentine steak salsa. Don't forget to put a fried egg on top of that steak, please.

Argentine beef truly does have a special flavor, and is probably similar to what the early American cowboys ate. Most Argentinian beef is "free-range," fed on natural pasture grasses with no antibiotics or other additives. This results in lighter marbling than in American beef, which is from steers that are generally fattened on corn in a feedlot before being slaughtered. There are other differences as well. Thick cuts of Argentine beef seem to puff up during grilling, and the meat has a slightly sweet gaminess that pleases some people and not others.

Until 1997, it was impossible to find Argentinian steaks in the United States. Various reasons were cited for the ban, including the danger of hoof-and-mouth

OPPOSITE: A WAITER CONTEMPLATES THE ARRIVAL OF HIS CUSTOMER'S ORDER; ASPARAGUS SPEARS WILL SOON BE ENHANCED WITH HOLLANDAISE SAUCE; NEW POTATOES READY FOR THE FLAME; AND A WAITER PUTS THE FINISHING TOUCHES ON HIS SERVICE, SECONDS BEFORE IT REACHES THE HUNGRY CUSTOMER.

disease, but politics, as usual, was the more likely reason. Now those politics have changed, and the United States allows twenty thousand tons (18,000t) of Argentine beef into the country each year. Most of it is sold by Argentine restaurants and specialty butchers.

These establishments usually pair the meat with wine made from Malbec grapes, a Bordeaux variety that has taken hold in the vineyards of Argentina; Catena, Weinert, and Navarra Correas are good vintners of this variety. Argentina also exports wines made from Torrontes grapes, which originally came from Spain, but have been cultivated in Argentina for over three centuries. Great wines, especially Cabernet and Merlot, also come from the Mendoza Valley, near where the international jet set likes to play. Argentine wine has a different character than Californian and French wines of the same grapes because most of the Argentine vineyards don't use oak casks to age their wine. The result is a fruity, refreshing flavor that goes surprisingly well with steak.

ABOVE: IT'S HARD TO FIND ROOM FOR DESSERT AFTER POLISHING OFF A SMITH & WOLLENSKY STEAK, BUT WITH OFFERINGS LIKE THE CHOCOLATE BASKET IN RASPBERRY SAUCE, LOTS OF CUSTOMERS MANAGE. **OPPOSITE**: HUNDREDS OF SIRLOINS ARE SERVED UP EVERY DAY AT SMITH & WOLLENSKY'S FLAGSHIP RESTAURANT ON MANHATTAN'S EAST SIDE.

BEEF CUTS

As with most things in life, a little knowledge of beef will increase your pleasure. To get more satisfaction from your carnivorous explorations, spend a little time learning about the various types of steaks available. Most steak cuts come from the rib, short loin, and sirloin sections of the animal, while roasts come from the end. Here are the main steak cuts, and the best ways to use them.

TENDERLOIN

Not surprisingly, given its name, this cut is often smooth enough to slice with a butter knife. It is pure beef, with no bone, and the high cost reflects this no-waste package. You may have seen an uncut tenderloin in a specialty butcher shop: it looks like a foot-and-a-half-long (45cm) tube of beautiful meat. Sometimes chefs or barbecue fanatics will cook a whole tenderloin and slice it for a large group, for a beef eating experience of unparalleled luxury. Sometimes the tenderest three-inch (7.6cm) section is cut out of the center to make Châteaubriand. But usually the tenderloin is cut into one-inch-thick (2.5cm), six- to twelve-ounce (170 to 340g) steaks called tenderloins or filets mignons. Of course, Smith & Wollensky's filets are larger than the norm, at one and a half inches (3.8cm) thick. These steaks can be wrapped in bacon and grilled for classic American service, panfried in a few drops of very hot oil, or even coated with peppercorns and drizzled with an au poivre sauce for a spicy treat.

T-BONES

In movies, when that crusty old cowpoke walks bow-legged into the saloon after a few months out on the range mending fences, spooning beans, and drinking gritty unfiltered coffee, he says to the waitress, "I'll have the T-bone, ma'am." The T-bone is a sort of rough-and-tumble, he-man steak, although certainly women have been known to enjoy it, too. While saddled with this no-frills image, the T-bone is truly one of the more elegant steaks, combining as it does a portion of the tenderloin and a portion of the top loin, separated by a nice-looking bone.

PORTERHOUSE

This is the steak of legend, the most pervasive being that it was named after the porter houses, or coach stops, that welcomed travelers in nineteenth-century America. It is said that this cut first became popular in New York City when the keeper of a porter house, Martin Morrison, started serving it to his guests. The steak comes from the short loin of the steer, and, like the T-bone, it has both top loin and tenderloin meat, although its tenderloin portion is a little bit larger. The porterhouse is great broiled or panfried, sliced thin or eaten on the bone.

BEEF CUTS

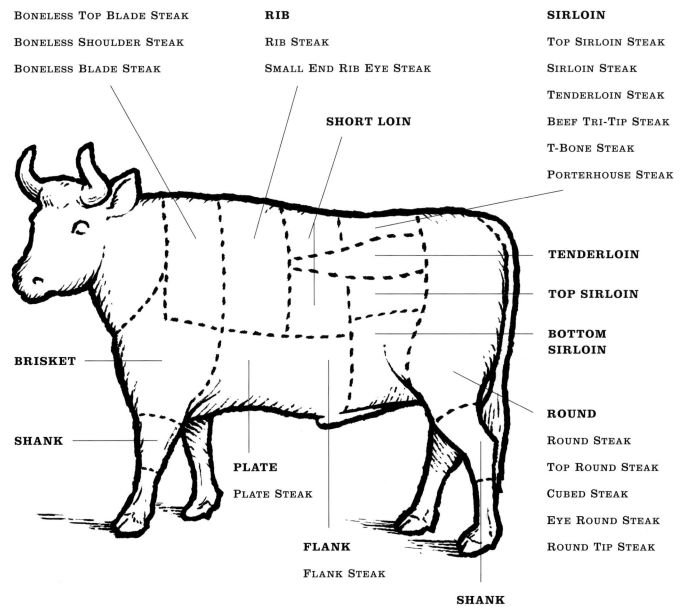

CHUCK

CHUCK EYE STEAK

BONELESS TOP BLADE STEAK

BONELESS SHOULDER STEAK

BONELESS BLADE STEAK

RIB

RIB STEAK

SMALL END RIB EYE STEAK

SHORT LOIN

SIRLOIN

TOP SIRLOIN STEAK

SIRLOIN STEAK

TENDERLOIN STEAK

BEEF TRI-TIP STEAK

T-BONE STEAK

PORTERHOUSE STEAK

TENDERLOIN

TOP SIRLOIN

**BOTTOM
SIRLOIN**

ROUND

ROUND STEAK

TOP ROUND STEAK

CUBED STEAK

EYE ROUND STEAK

ROUND TIP STEAK

BRISKET

SHANK

PLATE

PLATE STEAK

FLANK

FLANK STEAK

SHANK

The writer O. Henry was the first person to use the term filet (boneless) mignon (small), in his book

The Four Million, to describe a steak cut from the beef tenderloin.

OPPOSITE: THE PERFECT ARC OF A RIB STEAK MAKES A HUNGRY PERSON REACH FOR THE KNIFE AND GIVE THANKS FOR A GOOD MEAL TO COME. **ABOVE**: TOMMY HART (STANDING) AND VICTOR CHAVEZ (SEATED, RIGHT) HAVE BEEN WITH SMITH & WOLLENSKY SINCE THE DAY IT OPENED. DANNY KISSANE (SEATED, LEFT) HAS BEEN WITH THE RESTAURANT FOR EIGHTEEEN YEARS.

STRIP

Also called the top loin, this steak is most closely associated with two of our loveliest cities. In Kansas City, they often call it the New York strip steak. And in New York, it's sometimes called the Kansas City strip steak. Go figure. What doesn't vary is the fact that this cut comes from the second most tender muscle in the steer. Usually served boneless, it is an especially juicy cut, which gives it a lot of flavor. It is usually broiled until it gets a nice crust—although the broiler has to be very hot to do this well. The crust and the juicy flavor make this the second most popular steak in America, after the tenderloin steak. This is the perfect cut for steak and eggs.

RIB

Rib steaks would make a caveman feel right at home. Often huge and bloody and very high in fat, they are the cut for meat-eaters in the mood for a good, rich, beefy-flavored feed. At Smith & Wollensky, the prime rib is roasted in all its glory, and only trimmed a little before cooking. Once it's a perfect rare to medium rare, dinner is served. Each nearly two-pound (0.9kg) portion is sliced off the bone and served pink on the inside with a nice fatty crust on the outside. No one ever leaves the table hungry after eating a portion of rib steak.

RIB EYE

This superb steak is cut from the rib, the same meat used for prime rib. But the butcher trims away the fat and bone, leaving a perfect, tender portion that's great for grilling or broiling. It's a little chewier than a filet mignon, but every bit as luxurious.

SIRLOIN

Did the name of this steak arise when a king or queen liked the cut so much that it was dubbed "Sir Loin"? Everyone from King Henry II to King Charles II and even Queen Victoria has been credited with naming this steak, but it is doubtful that any English monarch would have sullied the image of the crown by knighting a piece of bloody meat. There's another explanation—the name is derived from the French word for top of the loin: *surlonge*. Some sirloins come

COMMON STEAK NAMES

The popular names given to different cuts of meat can vary from region to region, although the labels in supermarkets are consistent across the country. Here is a breakdown of frequently used steak names.

THE CUT	COMMON NAMES
PORTERHOUSE	Porterhouse steak
T-BONE	T-bone steak
STRIP	Strip steak, Kansas City strip, New York strip, hotel-style sirloin steak, club sirloin steak
TOP SIRLOIN BUTT STEAK	Boneless sirloin butt steak, sirloin butt steak
TENDERLOIN STEAK	Filet mignon, Tender steak, filet steak, filet de boeuf
RIB EYE	Delmonico steak, filet steak, Spencer steak, beauty steak

with flat bones, some with roundish bones, and some are topless. It all depends on how you like them—but every steak-eater likes some kind of sirloin.

GRILLING HABITS

Grilling is the traditional method for preparing steaks, with important precedents in legend and lore. The cowboys of the old West loved nothing more than to roast a steer over an open fire during a long cattle drive, serving the meat with beans, maybe some fry bread, and if they were lucky, a little coffee. The gauchos of the Argentine pampas developed similar traditions, roasting up huge slabs of fresh beef. And almost every weekend in the United States, hundreds of thousands of households wheel out the

ABOVE: SMITH & WOLLENSKY FOUNDER ALAN STILLMAN IS ALSO A CONNOISSEUR OF ANTIQUES; THIS EAGLE-TOPPED MORTAR AND PESTLE MAY ONCE HAVE POUNDED OUT HERBS FOR A MARINADE.

Americans eat more than 225 million steak sandwiches a year.

barbecue grill and continue the American cowboy tradition by laying some juicy steaks over the coals. On one of the busiest summer holiday weekends, Memorial Day, three in four households in the United States fire up the grill, and about half of them cook steaks. The traditional cuts—T-bone, rib eye, and sirloin—are the most popular for grilling. But filet mignon, New York strip, round steak, and flank steak also occupy their share of real estate over the charcoal.

According to a survey by the National Cattlemen's Beef Association, American grilling preferences, from favorite to least favorite, are:

PORTERHOUSE/T-BONE STEAK

RIB EYE STEAK

SIRLOIN STEAK

FILET MIGNON

NEW YORK STRIP STEAK

TOP ROUND STEAK

FLANK STEAK

CHUCK STEAK

LONDON BROIL

More than 60 percent of these steaks are treated to a marinade before they are laid on the grill. The rest are served plain and simple, with only the natural flavor of the steak to carry the day. Summer holiday weekends are the favorite times to grill.

LESS WORK, MORE BEEF

By one measure, the price of steak has actually gone down in the last eighty years. That might be shocking news to people who are used to thinking that everything costs more because of inflation. Sure, you have to unfold a few extra dollars to buy a pound of filet mignon now than you would have back in 1916—but according to economists W. Michael Cox and Richard Alm, it takes less work to be able to buy that pound of steak. In 1997, the Federal Reserve Bank in Dallas published a report by Cox and Alm suggesting that the real cost of living in America has gone down. The two authors chose as their fixed standard the number of work hours required to buy a certain item. Looking back over time, and determining the average hourly wage for non-managerial workers, they found some startling results: a pound of beef, which cost the equivalent of thirty minutes of a person's workday in 1916, cost only six minutes' work in 1997. The lower cost is probably due to increased supply, since modern livestock-raising techniques have made the U.S. cattle industry more efficient.

WHAT MAKES GREAT TASTE?

Three things contribute most to the taste of a steak: the age of the animal when slaughtered, the fat content, and how long the steak is aged.

AGE OF THE ANIMAL

The older the steer, the more flavorful the steaks, although very old animals will be too tough to eat, no matter how good they taste. The USDA considers any beef animal over thirty months of age to be too old for prime or choice grades. Many animals are slaughtered at twelve to fourteen months, although their flavor would benefit from a little more maturity.

FAT

Fat is good—not the big strips you trim off the edges and toss away, but the marbling that is visible in the meat. The more marbling, the more tender and juicy the steak. While the steak is cooking, the fat melts and spreads through the meat, holding in the water-soluble proteins that give the meat a lot of its flavor and fragrance.

AGING

Dry-aged steak, cut from beef that has hung in a cool room for two to four weeks, is the most flavorful beef because the aging concentrates the distinctive flavor of the meat. It is very difficult to find, however, and it is expensive because the aging process can make the meat shrink by more than 20 percent.

AGING STEAKS

The secret to a superb steak, rather than just a good steak, lies in the aging process. A fresh steak from a newly slaughtered animal just isn't the same as a steak that has been properly aged. Aged steaks—that

OPPOSITE: THE DRY-AGING PROCESS BREAKS DOWN TISSUE WITHIN THE STEAKS, MAKING THEM MORE TENDER AND FLAVORFUL. THESE RACKS WILL BE TRIMMED AND PORTIONED THE MORNING BEFORE THEY ARE SERVED.

have been "ripened" by the passing of time—taste better and cut more easily.

Smith & Wollensky steaks are "dry-aged," which is the most time-consuming and expensive way to cure a good steak. It is worth all the effort, though, because dry-aged steaks have a beefy taste that just can't be matched by other methods. The steaks aren't quite as moist as unaged meat, but they have a more intense and complex aroma. Dry-aging most closely

HOW TENDER IS MY STEAK?

Here's how Texas A & M University ranked steak cuts for their tenderness:

VERY TENDER

FILET MIGNON, OR TENDERLOIN

TENDER

TOP LOIN, OR STRIP

T-BONE

PORTERHOUSE

RIB STEAK

MODERATELY TENDER

CHUCK EYE

ROUND TIP

TOP SIRLOIN

replicates the original methods for curing steaks used by the cowboys and other historic steak lovers to make their meat taste great. Back in the days of the cattle drives, meat was aged in cool cellars or simply in the shade, but these days we cure meat in refrigerators at thirty-two to thirty-six degrees Fahrenheit (0° to 2° C) with circulating air to minimize the risk of bacteria.

The cattle used for Smith & Wollensky steaks are usually raised in western states such as Texas, Oklahoma, and Nebraska. They're slaughtered in the West, too, and cut into large sections before being brought east. Smith & Wollensky uses mostly the loin and rib sections, which are the source of the most desirable steaks, including the rib, T-bone, porterhouse, top loin, sirloin, and filet mignon. These sections are shipped in refrigerated trucks and delivered to the restaurants about ten days after the cattle have been processed. But that's only the beginning of the slow Smith & Wollensky aging process.

When the rib sections arrive at the restaurant, an assistant butcher writes the date on a piece of beige paper, and sticks it onto the meat with a sharpened dowel. The meat at this point has a three-quarter-inch (2cm) layer of fat over the top, and quite a bit of fat surrounding the rib bones. This is left on while it is aged. The sections are stacked on slat-wood shelves in a gigantic walk-in refrigerator that is kept at about thirty-two degrees Fahrenheit (0°C). Walking into a Smith & Wollensky meat locker is a real eye-opener—hundreds of rib and loin portions rest on the shelves in various stages of curing. The newest sections have the bright red color you're accustomed to seeing in grocery stores. As they age, however, they slowly take on a darker patina, which indicates that the muscle fibers are breaking down, giving the meat a richer, beefier flavor. After three to four weeks, the meat is ready. While the steak will still be soft to the touch, it will have developed a moldy crust, which means it is cured. During this process the meat shrinks by more than 20 percent due to water loss, which adds to the cost of producing such great steaks.

The science behind aging beef is based on enzymes in the muscles. As the meat sits in the cooler, natural tissue enzymes called "proteases" break down certain proteins in the muscle fibers, or "myofibrils." This breakdown tenderizes the ribs and loins. It all happens much more quickly in the first few days after slaughter, and slows down considerably after seven days. That's why the more common way of aging steaks—called wet-aging—tenderizes and flavors meat, but not as sublimely as dry-aging.

Wet-aged meat didn't become widespread until the 1970s, when a company called Iowa Beef developed methods for shipping meat around the country in vacuum packages. The process, because it was cheaper and easier, really put the kibosh on dry-aged beef, making it more of a specialty item. Wet-aged meat is packaged in airtight bags in the refrigerator until it reaches the store, about seven to ten days after slaughter, keeping most of the moisture in the meat. It bastes in its own juices, thus the term "wet-aged." (This technique is also used for Smith & Wollensky's filets mignons, which the chefs believe taste better wet-aged than dry-aged.) A wet-aged steak can be just as tender as the dry-aged variety, but it will most likely have more of a bloody flavor, and less of a subtle beefy taste.

A word of advice: don't try dry-aging your own steaks at home. Amateurs without the right equipment and knowledge run the risk of contracting foodborne illnesses from improperly cured meat.

MAKING THE GRADE

All steaks must meet federal inspection requirements, according to a law passed in 1906, and the responsibility for grading the quality of steaks is placed on the packing houses. These meat producers hire United States Department of Agriculture workers to grade their meat, and so indicate to the consumer what he or she is buying. The grade depends on the age of the

STEAK WOLLENSKY

SERVES: 4

PREPARATION TIME: 30 minutes

INGREDIENTS

4 16-OUNCE DRY-AGED PRIME SIRLOIN STEAKS

6 OUNCES FRESH MUSHROOMS, SLICED

2 SMALL ONIONS, SLICED

SEPARATELY IN 3/8-INCH ROUNDS

1 STICK BUTTER

1/4 CUP BUTTERMILK

1/4 CUP FLOUR

VEGETABLE OIL FOR FRYING

INSTRUCTIONS

Clarify the butter: heat the butter over medium heat in a small pan until bubbles form. Do not brown. Remove from heat and slowly pour the clear top layer of butter out of the pan into a small bowl, discarding the white solids in the bottom of the pan. Cook the steaks (preferably on a grill) at high heat for about 12 to 15 minutes. If you prepare them medium rare, let them rest for a few minutes before slicing them. Meanwhile, sauté the mushrooms in half the butter at high heat and keep warm. Sauté one onion in the remaining butter at high heat and keep warm. Make onion rings with the remaining onion: Separate the rings and sprinkle them with buttermilk. Dust them with flour and fry them in hot oil until golden brown. Keep them warm. Slice the steaks and arrange them over a bed of sautéed onions. Top them with some sautéed mushrooms and add onion rings as a garnish.

OPPOSITE: THE VENERABLE PORTERHOUSE TOOK ITS NAME FROM THE "PORTER HOUSES," OR COACH STOPS, WHERE STEAKS WERE SERVED TO NINETEENTH-CENTURY TRAVELERS.

New York strip steaks are more commonly served in the Western states—they're hard to find in New York!

animal at slaughter, the amount of marbling in the lean meat of the rib eye at the twelfth rib, and the meat's color and general attractiveness.

While there are eight different grades of beef, the only ones you are likely to see in the supermarket are "prime," "choice," and "select." "Prime" is a truly special grade because only 2 percent of meat sold in the United States earns this mark of distinction. Most of this is sold to restaurants, although some supermarkets carry it. About 45 percent is graded "choice," the most widely available grade in supermarkets, and 27 percent is graded "select."

Another word of advice: it is not unusual these days to walk into a gigantic grocery store and find steaks labeled "Butcher's Prime," "Market Choice," "Lean Select," and other fancy names. While it is easy to be fooled by these designations, try to be alert. These are fantasy names, totally meaningless distinctions the supermarket has given to ungraded steaks— meat that is fit for human consumption, but not guaranteed to be much better than that. The only legal grades are accompanied by the letters USDA on the label. Remember, meat only has to pass a general inspection—it isn't required to be graded.

GROCERY STEAKS

There can be a huge difference between steaks sold at different grocery stores. The first step toward insuring that your steak will be as delicious as it should be is choosing a good grocer or butcher. That means someone who does a lot of business.

It's worth going to a store with a full parking lot. Even if the walk to the entrance is long, the crowd ensures a high meat turnover, meaning the meat will be fresh. That lonely store with only one car in the lot might seem convenient, but there is probably a reason no one shops there.

Your best bet is a store with its own butchering staff, preferably people who are available to speak about the various cuts in the case. They'll take more pride than butchers who are hidden in a back room, or worse yet, in another location altogether.

When picking a portion of wet-aged beef, look for steaks that are either bright red or dark purplish-red. The darker color comes from vacuum packing, which keeps the steak in an oxygen-free environment for freshness. Once you open the package and expose the steak to the air, it will gradually

ABOVE: WHERE WILL THE ARROW LAND? EXOTIC ANTIQUES AND UNIQUE WORKS OF ART LEND ATMOSPHERE TO ALL SMITH & WOLLENSKY RESTAURANTS.

turn dark red, and then bright red. Avoid steaks that have gray or brown blotches. Why eat meat that is not perfect?

Touch the steaks through their wrapping, or ask the butcher to let you feel a steak before you buy it. Good ones will be firm to the touch, without any softness. Make sure the steak is cold, and that the package isn't torn.

Do not buy steaks that are swimming in juices; this might mean they were not handled properly, or were stored too long. Double-check the expiration date to make sure your steaks are fresh.

Always make your steak purchases toward the end of your shopping, after you have picked out everything else in the store that you need. That way your steaks won't have time to warm up on the trip

STORING STEAKS

Here is a list of safe storage periods for refrigerated and frozen beef.

TYPE OF BEEF	REFRIGERATOR 35°F (1.7°C) to 40°F (4.4°C)	FREEZER 0°F (-17.8°C) or colder
RAW WHOLE STEAKS	3 to 4 days	up to 12 months
RAW CHOPPED STEAK	1 to 2 days	up to 4 months
LEFTOVER COOKED STEAK	3 to 4 days	up to 3 months
VACUUM PACKED	consult package	consult package

you don't trust the wrapping, put a layer of plastic wrap around the steaks or put them in a plastic bag before placing them in the refrigerator. If the steaks are vacuum-packed, check the label for storage instructions.

If you plan to keep your steaks for more than four days, store them in the freezer at zero degrees Fahrenheit (-17.8° C) or colder. The faster the better when freezing beef—slow freezing leads to larger ice crystals, which tend to rupture muscle tissues and affect the taste and texture of the steaks. The store's plastic wrapping is sufficient for steaks that will be eaten within two weeks. To avoid freezer burn on steaks that are to be stored for longer periods, wrap them again, in freezer paper or heavy-duty aluminum foil.

Thaw the steaks by placing them in the refrigerator the day before you plan to feast; it will usually take fifteen to twenty-four hours for them to defrost. Never thaw them at room temperature because that could lead to unhealthy bacterial growth.

home. You should not leave steaks unrefrigerated for more than about thirty minutes.

It is important to refrigerate or freeze your beef as soon as you get home. If you plan to eat your steaks within four days, and they are well wrapped in transparent film, just put them right in the refrigerator. If the butcher put them in paper, or

HOW MUCH TO BUY

People buy different amounts of steak for different occasions. Clearly, extra-large portions like those served at Smith & Wollensky won't grace the home dining table day after day. The U.S. Department of

Agriculture suggests serving three-ounce (85g) portions, although that might seem small to some people. Generally, four ounces (115g) of boneless raw steak will yield three ounces (85g) of cooked, trimmed meat, and eight ounces (225g) will yield six ounces (170g). Here are some guidelines from the National Cattlemen's Beef Association:

STEAK	YIELD *
CHUCK SHOULDER	3.5
CHUCK TOP BLADE	3
FLANK	4
PORTERHOUSE/T-BONE	2.5
RIB	2.5
RIB EYE	3
TENDERLOIN	4
TOP LOIN, BONELESS	3.75
TOP ROUND	4
TOP SIRLOIN, BONELESS	3.5
ROUND TIP, THIN CUT	4

*in 3-ounce (85g) portions per pound (454g) of raw meat

GET YOUR ZINC HERE

The effects of zinc on the human body have been debated endlessly, and continue to be a fertile area for scientific study. The mineral has been thought to guard against prostate problems, colds, impotence, cancer, and a host of other illnesses. Perhaps the most documented advantage of zinc is in the prevention of colds in children. What is without dispute is that zinc is lacking in many Americans' diets, especially those of women and young children.

Zinc is a delicate mineral, and the foods you eat can either enhance or diminish how well your body uses this nutrient. Whole grains contain high levels of zinc, but not in a form that is easily absorbed by the body. Researchers have shown that eating beef can actually help a person absorb zinc from other foods. And not only does beef increase the bioavailability of zinc in other foods, but it also contains high levels of the mineral itself, in an easily absorbed form. Some studies have shown that the zinc found in beef is absorbed by the body four times more easily than the zinc found in breakfast cereals, which are a common source of it.

OPPOSITE: MEN AND WOMEN GATHER UNDER THIS GRAND PIECE OF ART IN THE BAR IN THE EARLY EVENING TO SHARE TALES AND DRINKS, AND TO WHET THEIR APPETITES IN PREPARATION FOR THE MEAL TO COME.

Total beef production in the United States is about twenty-five billion pounds a year.

PUMPING MORE IRON

Steak is one of the best foods for curing a very serious illness. Anemia, or iron deficiency, afflicts more people in the United States than any other nutritional problem, according to the United States Center for Disease Control. Ten percent of women between twelve and forty-nine years of age suffer from anemia, as do 30 percent of poor women who are pregnant, and almost 10 percent of children between one and three years old. The problem can cause learning disabilities and behavior problems, and lead children to score lower than normal on IQ tests and perform poorly in school. In pregnant women, it can lead to premature birth and low birth weight.

According to the experts, the way to prevent anemia is through a diet rich in foods with high iron content—such as steak. Beef contains large amounts of heme iron, which is more easily absorbed by the body than the irons found in vegetarian foods like grains, vegetables, and fruits. According to the National Cattlemen's Beef Association, three ounces (85g) of cooked sirloin steak has the same amount of iron as a medium-sized baked potato (about 2.8 milligrams), but the steak has two and a half times as much heme iron as the potato.

Curiously, beef also has the effect of enhancing the body's ability to absorb non-heme iron from plants. So if you eat your potato with a steak, you'll get a significantly larger iron boost from the spud than you would if you ate it without beef. Sadly, many people who stand to benefit from an iron-rich diet are likely to avoid beef out of a belief that it is high in calories and fat. But the truth is that the leanest cuts have the same iron as fatty cuts.

ABOVE: CHOCOLATE LAYER CAKE IS A WELL-EARNED INDULGENCE AT THE END OF THE MEAL.
SMITH & WOLLENSKY PASTRY CHEFS ALWAYS HAVE AN ENTICING ARRAY OF RICH DESSERTS ON HAND.

WHAT'S IN A STEAK

Based on U.S. Department of Agriculture sources. Figures are based on three-ounce (85g) portions of lean, broiled steak, with less than one-quarter inch (6mm) of fat.

CUT	CALORIES	PROTEIN	TOTAL FAT	SAT. FAT	IRON	SODIUM	CHOLESTEROL
TENDERLOIN	179	24g	9g	3.2g	3mg	54mg	71mg
TOP LOIN	176	24g	8g	3.1g	2.1mg	58mg	65mg
PORTERHOUSE, CHOICE	183	22g	10g	3.4g	2.6mg	59mg	59mg
T-BONE	174	23g	9g	3.1g	2.7mg	60mg	50mg
RIB EYE	191	24g	10g	4g	2.2mg	59mg	68mg
TOP SIRLOIN	166	26g	6g	2.4g	2.9mg	56mg	76mg
FLANK	176	23g	9g	3.7g	2.2mg	71mg	57mg

TRIMMING FAT

It is a good idea to trim your steak, but only after you cook it. The fatty ribbons clinging to a good steak help give it a great flavor as it cooks. But it is not necessary, nor is it recommended, to eat much fat, especially if you are watching your waistline or your cholesterol level. You can lay waste to a significant number of calories, as much as 50 percent of the fat, and a good amount of cholesterol just by trimming all the visible fat from the steak before you eat it. If you are more concerned about fat than flavor, trim the

OPPOSITE: THE VARIETY OF FOODS SERVED AT SMITH & WOLLENSKY SURPRISES SOME CUSTOMERS WHO COME SOLELY IN SEARCH OF STEAK. BUT THEY ARE NEVER DISAPPOINTED, BECAUSE STEAK, AFTER ALL, IS THE RESTAURANT'S NUMBER ONE BUSINESS.

steak before you cook it. That will prevent any of the fat from being soaked up by the lean meat as it cooks.

IS IT DONE YET?

There are three different ways to tell if a steak is done: look at it, touch it, or measure its temperature. The scale of doneness goes like this:

RARE—Bright red center and pink near the outside edges.

MEDIUM RARE—Pink center, and the outside edges are slightly brown.

MEDIUM—Faint pink center, and the rest is brown.

WELL DONE—The meat is brown from the inside to the outside.

The easiest way to tell if a steak is done is by using the visual method: if the steak is boneless, use a knife to make a small slit in the center to check the color of the meat. If the steak has a bone, check the meat near the bone, not the center of the steak. But some people don't like to cut into a steak before they serve it, because some of the juices inevitably run out.

An alternative is to use an instant thermometer, which checks the internal temperature of the steak in seconds. Note that instant thermometers cannot be left in the meat while it cooks. Some stores also sell electric thermometers with a display that shows the level of doneness—rare, medium, or well—of the steak. The temperature probe is inserted into the steak and connected by a wire to a monitor resting on the kitchen counter. As the steak cooks, the monitor shows how far along it is. An alarm goes off when the meat is at the desired temperature, or doneness.

The U.S. Department of Agriculture recommends these internal temperatures for steaks cooked at home:

MEDIUM RARE: 145°F (63°C)

MEDIUM: 160°F (70°)

WELL DONE: 170°F (77°)

More experienced chefs, including all the grill cooks at Smith & Wollensky restaurants, combine the visual method with the touch method. Touching for doneness takes practice, but in time the tension on the

'95 Opus One $119.00

Tomato Bisque

Broccoli ~ String Beans

Shrimp Cocktail

Filet Mignon

Pan Roasted Mahi Mahi

Grilled Chicken Breast

Lemon Pepper Tuna

Hashed Browns

Bourbon Pecan Pie

FILET AU POIVRE

SERVES: 4

PREPARATION TIME: 20 minutes

INGREDIENTS

1 1/2 STICKS BUTTER

1 CUP CRACKED BLACK PEPPERCORNS

4 16-OUNCE PRIME FILETS MIGNONS

BOTTLED AU POIVRE SAUCE

INSTRUCTIONS

Preheat the oven to 350°F. In a cast iron sauté pan, heat the butter. Place
the peppercorns on a plate and press each filet firmly onto the peppercorns
on both sides. Sauté the filets in the butter at high heat for 2 minutes on
each side and finish in the oven for about 15 to 18 minutes until medium
rare. Serve on a pool of au poivre sauce.

**Meat and potatoes have gone the way of the drive-in movie. Only 22 percent of Americans serve meat plain,
accompanied by side dishes. Instead, casseroles and other combinations predominate. Still, meat is the most
common protein served at dinner.**

ABOVE: You can't beat this waiter's sense of humor. **OPPOSITE**: The upstairs dining room in New York is drenched with sun from skylights and windows.

surface of the steak will let you know how far along it is in the cooking process. Fortunately, you don't have to waste dozens of steaks trying to perfect this method. Instead, you can practice on your own hands.

FOR RARE STEAKS

Let your hand hang, loose and relaxed, from the wrist. With the index finger of your other hand, touch the flesh between the thumb and index finger. It is soft and spongy—which is what a rare steak feels like.

FOR MEDIUM RARE STEAKS

Keeping your hand loose, make a fist. With your

other index finger, touch the same spot between your thumb and index finger. You will feel a little more resistance. That is what a medium-rare steak feels like.

FOR MEDIUM STEAKS

Clench your fist tightly. When you touch the same area, it feels firm—like a medium steak.

FOR WELL-DONE STEAKS

Cook the meat a while longer than a medium steak. Don't bother practicing on your hand—just remove the steak from the heat before it burns.

MY STEAK JUST ISN'T AS GOOD

———◆———

The waiter seats you at one of Smith & Wollensky's cloth-covered tables. There is a beautiful picture of a reclining nude above your table, an antique toy fire engine in a case mounted nearby, and quite a number of grand bottles of wine on display. It seems like a nice place, and when they bring your steak it looks better than any steak you've ever cooked at home. Not surprisingly, it tastes great, too. Why is this steak different from the ones you cook on the backyard barbecue? Probably because restaurant kitchens have extremely hot grills that sear the steak and give it a crusty, flavorful surface in a way that home broilers and barbecue grills just can't duplicate because of their lower heat. Also, the steaks used at Smith & Wollensky are dry-aged for up to a month, which adds a deep, beefy flavor. You can come close to experiencing this great flavor at home by ordering a dry-aged steak directly from Smith & Wollensky, to be shipped to your barbecue pit by overnight mail.

HOW TO BROIL A STEAK

———◆———

Smith & Wollensky's kitchens broil their steaks to achieve a charred, flavorful crust. But broiling isn't among the easiest ways to prepare meat (the easiest way is by ordering off a menu and letting someone else do the cooking). As the legendary food writer Anthelme Brillat-Savarin wrote: "We can learn to be cooks, but we must be born knowing how to roast."

The key to good broiling is an extremely high temperature, which is also what makes broiling a steak so difficult. Glowing coals and electric coils both reach about 2,000°F (1,090°C), and a gas flame can get as hot as 3,000°F (1,650°C). The high heat makes a steak brown quickly and thoroughly, which gives it a great flavor. But in the process, the inside of the meat sometimes doesn't have time to absorb enough heat through its water molecules to cook—and you end up with a charred piece of meat that is still cold and blue in the center. The trick is to keep your steak just far enough from the heat source—the flame, electric coil, or coals—to sear it, while keeping it on the heat long enough to cook the meat. And since that optimal distance varies

OPPOSITE: STEAK AND POTATOES. WHAT COULD BE MORE AMERICAN— OR MORE ENTICING—THAN THAT TIME-HONORED COMBINATION?

People in the southern Atlantic states, such as the Carolinas, Georgia, and Florida, eat many more steaks in restaurants than people from other parts of the country.

PAGE 88: A CUP OF COFFEE MAKES A GOOD PICK-ME-UP FOR A DINER GORGED ON BEEF.

PAGE 89: MOST STEAK-EATERS OPT FOR RED WINE, BUT THERE ARE PLENTY OF OPTIONS FOR THOSE WHO PREFER A GOOD WHITE. **ABOVE**: IF YOU CAN'T MAKE IT TO A SMITH & WOLLENSKY, YOU CAN TRY TO RE-CREATE THE EXPERIENCE AT HOME. SOME SMITH & WOLLENSKY STEAK SAUCE WILL ADD AUTHENTICITY.

from kitchen to kitchen, depending on the equipment, you'll have to experiment a little.

To broil a steak, you have to remember only three simple steps. Step one is the easiest: turn your oven on to broil and preheat it for ten minutes. It doesn't matter whether it is gas or electric. With an electric range, leave the door slightly ajar—most doors are designed to sit a few inches open (this will prevent the oven from heating up too much). You can leave gas range doors closed during broiling.

BROILING

CUT	THICKNESS/ WEIGHT	APPROXIMATE DISTANCE FROM HEAT	COOKING TIME (FOR MEDIUM RARE TO MEDIUM)
RIB EYE STEAK	3/4 inch (2cm)	2–3 inches (5–7.5cm)	8–10 minutes
	1 inch (2.5cm)	3–4 inches (7.5–10cm)	14–18 minutes
	1 1/2 inches (4cm)	3–4 inches (7.5–10cm)	21–27 minutes
RIB STEAK (small end)	3/4 inch (2cm)	2–3 inches (5–7.5cm)	9–12 minutes
	1 inch (2.5cm)	3–4 inches (7.5–10cm)	13–17 minutes
	1 1/2 inches (4cm)	3–4 inches (7.5–10cm)	24–31 minutes
PORTERHOUSE	3/4 inch (2cm)	2–3 inches (5–7.5cm)	10 – 13 minutes
			15 – 20 minutes
	1 1/2 inches (4cm)	3–4 inches (7.5–10cm)	27 – 32 minutes
TOP LOIN (boneless)	3/4 inch (2cm)	2–3 inches (5–7.5cm)	9–11 minutes
	1 inch (2.5cm)	3–4 inches (7.5–10cm)	13–17 minutes
	1 1/2 inches (4cm)	3–4 inches (7.5–10cm)	18–22 minutes
TENDERLOIN	1 inch (2.5cm)	2–3 inches (5–7.5cm)	13 – 16 minutes
	1 1/2 inches (4cm)	3–4 inches (7.5–10cm)	18–22 minutes
TOP SIRLOIN (boneless)	3/4 inch (2cm)	2–3 inches (5–7.5cm)	9–12 minutes
	1 inch (2.5cm)	3–4 inches (7.5–10cm)	16–21 minutes
	1 1/2 inches (4cm)	3–4 inches (7.5–10cm)	26–31 minutes
	2 inches (5cm)	3-4 inches (7.5–10cm)	34–39 minutes (turning occasionally)
FLANK (marinate first)	1 1/2 to 2 lb. (680–910g)	3 inches (7.5cm)	13–18 minutes
TOP ROUND (marinate first)	3/4 inch (2cm)	2–3 inches (5–7.5cm)	8 – 9 minutes
	1 inch (2.5cm)	2–3 inches (5–7.5cm)	16 – 18 minutes
	1 1/2 inch (4cm)	3–4 inches (7.5–10cm)	25 – 28 minutes
CHUCK SHOULDER (boneless, marinate first)	3/4 inch (2cm)	2–3 inches (5–7.5cm)	10–13 minutes
	1 inch (2.5cm)	3–4 inches (7.5–10cm)	16–21 minutes

Step two: take the steak from the refrigerator and season it to your taste, then put it directly onto the broiler pan.

Step three: Broil it to the doneness desired (see chart), turning only once. The chart times are for medium rare to medium steaks; adjust the cooking time according to other preferences.

ON THE GRILL

Grill aficionados have countless tricks of the trade, but really it is not all that complicated to make a steak taste great on a beautiful summer afternoon. If you start with the best steaks you can find, their flavor will carry the day. And note the following points of great grilling, to get the most out of your cut of meat.

First, try to have a little patience. More than a few great meals have been ruined by coals that were too hot and burned the steaks. Let the coals burn until they are covered with a light-gray ash. This will take about thirty minutes. Then spread them in a single layer across the bottom of the grill, and use your hand as a thermometer to check the temperature. When the coals are right for steaks, you should be able to hold your hand at cooking height over the coals for about four seconds, no more and no less. This is not a contest, so be careful not to burn yourself—it is very difficult to cut a steak with a bandaged hand.

Take your steak from the marinade, or if you are using a fresh steak, season it to taste with pepper or other spices (except salt, which should be added only after the beef has been seared) or nothing at all. With the grill resting close to the coals, place the steak directly over the heat.

If you are cooking with charcoal, use the times listed opposite, based on data from the National Cattlemen's Beef Association, as a reference. If you are using a gas grill, check the booklet that came with it for cooking times. Turn your steak occasionally, making sure

ABOVE: HE'S A STEAK STAR, AND HE KNOWS IT. TAKE HIS ADVICE, BECAUSE HE'S ALWAYS RIGHT.

ON THE GRILL

BEEF CUT	THICKNESS/ WEIGHT	COOKING TIME (MEDIUM RARE TO MEDIUM)
RIB EYE STEAK	3/4 inch (2cm)	6–8 minutes
	1 inch (2.5cm)	11–14 minutes
	1 1/2 inches (4cm)	17–22 minutes
PORTERHOUSE OR T-BONE	3/4 inch (2cm)	10–12 minutes
	1 inch (2.5cm)	14–16 minutes
	1 1/2 inches (4cm)	20–24 minutes
TOP LOIN (boneless)	3/4 inch (2cm)	10–12 minutes
	1 inch (2.5cm)	15–18 minutes
TENDERLOIN	1 inch (2.5cm)	13–15 minutes
	1 1/2 inches (4cm)	14–16 minutes
TOP SIRLOIN (boneless)	3/4 inch (2cm)	13–16 minutes
	1 inch (2.5cm)	17–21 minutes
	1 1/2 inches (4cm)	22–26 minutes
	2 inches (5cm)	28–33 minutes
FLANK (marinate first)	1 1/2 to 2 lb. (680–910g)	17–21 minutes
TOP ROUND (marinate first)	3/4 inch (2cm)	8–9 minutes
	1 inch (2.5cm)	16–18 minutes
	1 1/2 inch (4cm)	25–28 minutes
CHUCK SHOULDER (boneless, marinate first)	3/4 inch (2cm)	14–17 minutes
	1 inch (2.5cm)	16–20 minutes
CHUCK TOP BLADE (boneless)	1 inch (2.5cm)	18–22 minutes

Americans now eat about 64.4 pounds (29.2kg) of beef per person per year (boneless weight).

Compare that to 49.8 pounds (22.6kg) of pork, and 50.2 (22.8kg) pounds of chicken.

SMITH & WOLLENSKY HASH BROWNS

SERVES: 2

PREPARATION TIME: 15 minutes

INGREDIENTS

4 IDAHO POTATOES, BOILED
AND REFRIGERATED OVERNIGHT

1 SMALL GREEN PEPPER

1 SMALL ONION

4 TABLESPOONS BUTTER, CLARIFIED
(SEE STEAK WOLLENSKY)

1 TEASPOON HACOMAT SEASONING

SALT AND PEPPER TO TASTE

INSTRUCTIONS

Peel and dice the potatoes into small dice; set aside. Chop the green pepper and onion and sauté in the clarified butter until translucent. Add the potatoes and season with hacomat seasoning, and salt and pepper to taste. Cook at high heat without stirring until a golden-brown crust forms on the bottom. Flip and brown the other side. Serve.

Châteaubriand, a dish of broiled tenderloin served with béarnaise sauce, was created for the French writer and statesman Vicomte François-Auguste-René Châteaubriand by his chef Montmireil, during the reign of Napoleon.

PAN BROILING

CUT OF STEAK	THICKNESS	COOKING TIME (MEDIUM RARE TO MEDIUM)
RIB EYE	3/4 inch (2cm)	8–10 minutes
	1 inch (2.5cm)	12–15 minutes
PORTERHOUSE/T-BONE	3/4 inch (2cm)	11–13 minutes
	1 inch (2.5cm)	14–17 minutes
TOP LOIN (boneless)	3/4 inch (2cm)	10–12 minutes
	1 inch (2.5cm)	12–15 minutes
TENDERLOIN	1/2 inch (1.25cm)	3 1/2–5 1/2 minutes
	3/4 inch (2cm)	10–13 minutes
	1 inch (2.5cm)	10–13 minutes
TOP SIRLOIN (boneless)	3/4 inch (2cm)	11–12 minutes

to position it so the grill leaves a nice crosshatched pattern on the meat. The grill should be covered only when cooking steaks that are 1 1/2 inches (4cm) thick or more. Otherwise, cook them uncovered.

These times are for preparing medium rare to medium steaks. Adjust the cooking time according to other preferences.

PAN BROILING

It is not necessary to fire up the grill or oven broiler every time you want a steak. Try broiling it in a heavy skillet instead. (This works best for thin steaks.) Many people prefer a non-stick skillet, because no fat is necessary.

OPPOSITE: PRESSED TIN WALLS AND MARBLE-BACKED BOOTHS LEND THE NEW YORK RESTAURANT AN AIR OF HISTORY.

OPPOSITE: THE KITCHEN IS A FAST AND FURIOUS PLACE WHERE THE ACTION NEVER STOPS, FROM SLICING TO SAUTEING TO WASHING UP. THE CHEF FREQUENTLY SCRUTINIZES ORDERS BEFORE WAITERS BRING THE PLATES INTO THE DINING ROOM. **BELOW:** COCONUT CAKE IS ARTFULLY SERVED WITH A YIN-YANG MOTIF IN CARAMEL. PORTION CONTROL? NO THANK YOU.

First, preheat the skillet for a few minutes over medium heat. If you are using a cast-iron or other skillet without a non-stick surface, season the surface with a small amount of olive oil. Then place the steak directly into the pan, uncovered, and cook it according to the times listed on p.96. Make sure the skillet is not too small—steaks need room or else steam builds up, hindering the browning process. Turn the steak only once, unless it is over 1 inch (2.5cm) thick, in which case you should turn it several times to make sure it is cooked on the inside without burning on the outside. If too much juice collects in the skillet during cooking, remove it with a spoon. When the steak is done, season it with salt and serve.

WOLLENSKY SALAD

SERVES: 2

PREPARATION TIME: 10 minutes

INGREDIENTS

1 IDAHO POTATO, CUBED

4 OZ. SLAB OF BACON, CUBED

1/2 CUP VEGETABLE OIL

1 HEAD ROMAINE LETTUCE,

WASHED AND CHOPPED

1/4 CUP OLIVE OIL

1/4 CUP VINEGAR

4 RED PEAR TOMATOES, HALVED

4 YELLOW PEAR TOMATOES, HALVED

1 BUNCH WATERCRESS, WASHED

2 FRESH MUSHROOMS, SLICED

INSTRUCTIONS

Fry the potatoes and bacon cubes in the vegetable oil and set aside. Toss the romaine with the olive oil and vinegar. Place the lettuce in a wooden bowl and top it with the remaining ingredients. Serve.

The word "steak" has several possible roots. It may be traced back to the Saxons, the Germanic people who brought their love of beef with them when they conquered England in the sixth century. The Saxons appreciated a good chunk of beef grilled on a stick over a campfire, and their word for this delicacy was "steik." In Old Norse, the word "steikja" referred to the process of roasting meat on a stake.

GENERAL GUIDELINES

If you're still nervous about cooking your steak, here are some general guidelines to follow, according to the chefs at Smith & Wollensky. The instructions are based on cooking a 3/4- to 1-inch-thick (2–2.5cm) steak, so adjust as necessary for the thickness of your meat.

First, heat your oiled skillet to a light smoking state, or let your broiler heat up to full heat. Keep the broiler door open a crack if it is electric.

To cook the steak to a "blueish," or almost raw, state, cook 30 seconds on each side, then repeat for 30 seconds on each side. The outside will be slightly charred, and the inside will be blueish-red.

For rare, cook 30 seconds per side, and then cook 1 1/2 to 2 minutes per side. The inside should be red when you cut it.

For medium, cook 30 seconds per side, and then 2 to 3 1/2 minutes per side, until the center is slightly pinkish.

For well-done, again, cook 30 seconds on each side and then cook each side again for 5 minutes. The steak will be brown on the inside.

PLAY IT SAFE

Like any perishable food, steaks can cause illness if they aren't cared for and handled properly. The Center for Disease Control says almost all foodborne illnesses could be prevented if people took better care in handling what they cook and eat. Experts from the CDC and the U.S. Food and Drug Administration offer the following tips for safe steaks:

◆ Don't buy steaks that have an expired "sell by" or "use by" date.

◆ If the meat case doesn't seem to be cooling the meat well, go to another store.

◆ Don't buy steaks whose packaging is ripped or torn.

◆ If the steak is frozen, it should be solid as a rock.

◆ Buy the steaks last, so they have less time to warm up in the cart.

◆ Once home, put the steaks in the coldest part of the refrigerator right away.

◆ Eat the steaks you buy within three to four days of purchase, or freeze them.

◆ Don't let the steak juices drip onto other foods in the refrigerator—putting the steak in a plastic bag

OPPOSITE: MEDIUM-RARE TRIPLE LAMB CHOPS INTERTWINED ON A PLATE.

Round and loin cuts of beef have about the same amount of fat as chicken breasts and thighs.

is a good idea, even if it is already wrapped.

◆ Use freezer bags, aluminum foil, or freezer wrap, even if the steak is already covered, before putting the meat in the freezer.

◆ Thaw the meat in the refrigerator, not out in the open or in warm water. This will take about twelve to fifteen hours.

◆ Remember to keep your work area and hands clean. Wash everything thoroughly with hot water, including the cutting board, utensils, sink, and your hands.

◆ Wash your hands before and after handling the steak. Don't use the same preparation surfaces, such as cutting boards, for the cooked meat after the raw meat, unless you wash them thoroughly with soap and water. To truly sanitize a surface, wash it with a solution of three teaspoons (15ml) bleach to one quart (1L) of warm water. Then rinse with clean hot water.

◆ Cough and sneeze away from the steaks.

◆ Always marinate steaks in the refrigerator. Use non-metallic containers, since the acids in most marinades can leach the metal out of a container, allowing it to enter your food.

◆ Don't brush or spread used marinade on cooked meat, or use it as a sauce, because it might have been contaminated by the raw meat. If you want to use it as a sauce, heat it to a rolling boil and let it boil for at least a minute. It would be safer to mix two batches of marinade, and use the "clean" one for the sauce.

◆ While hamburger should be cooked until it is no longer pink in the center, steak is safe eaten medium rare. Bacteria, which are found only on the surface of whole meat, get mixed into the meat when it is ground up. The surface bacteria are killed by the high heat used to cook a steak, but more cooking is required to kill the bacteria that may be lurking in hamburger.

◆ Super-thick steaks of two inches (5cm) or more should be checked with a meat thermometer and cooked until they are 160°F (71°C) inside. Insert the thermometer into the thickest part of the meat, away from the bone.

◆ Don't partially cook the steaks and then finish them off later. They will not taste as good, because they will have lost a lot of juice, and they also might breed bacteria.

OPPOSITE: THE CLASSIC T-BONE, IN THE OVERSIZED SMITH & WOLLENSKY EDITION.

No type of beef is more popular than steak, which makes up almost 20 percent of the beef served in North American homes.

◆ If you are grilling in the great outdoors, away from home, make sure to pack some cleaning wipes to wash your hands with after you handle the steaks, or take a bottle of clean water and a bar of soap.

◆ Don't leave cooked meat sitting at room temperature for more than two hours.

◆ Always use a fresh or well-washed plate to serve cooked meat. Do not return the meat to the platter that held it when it was raw.

PAGE 106: A CHEF CHECKS HIS PROGRESS. **PAGE 107:** THE INTENSE HEAT OF THE BROILERS GIVES SMITH & WOLLENSKY STEAKS THEIR PERFECTLY CHARRED CRUST. **ABOVE:** COOKING THE PERFECT STEAK REQUIRES EXPERIENCE, PATIENCE, AND THE SPECIAL UNDERSTANDING OF BEEF SHARED BY ONLY THE GREATEST CHEFS.

"The meats and fish to be found at Smith & Wollensky are top-quality stuff, served up in massive portions. The Smith & Wollensky scenario has been tailored to the expectations of the clientele."—*GOURMET* MAGAZINE

T A R T   T A T I N

SERVES: 6

PREPARATION TIME: 30 minutes

INGREDIENTS

1/2 CUP SUGAR

1 CUP WATER

8 RED DELICIOUS APPLES, PEELED, CORED

AND SLICED

4 TABLESPOONS UNSALTED BUTTER

2 TABLESPOONS LEMON JUICE

1 POUND PIE CRUST

(SEE RECIPE BELOW)

INSTRUCTIONS

Preheat the oven to 325°F. Boil the sugar, water, and lemon juice in a saucepan until the mixture is golden brown. Divide the caramel between 6 ramekins 1 1/2-inches high and 3 inches in diameter. Place the slices of each apple over the caramel in a ramekin. Bake for about 45 minutes. Remove from oven and let cool a bit. Roll out the pie crust to 1/4-inch thick. Cut 6 circles of the diameter of the ramekins. Cover each tart with a pie crust circle and bake again until the crust is golden brown. Remove from the oven and invert immediately on serving plates. Serve plain or with whipped cream.

PIE CRUST INGREDIENTS

2 STICKS UNSALTED BUTTER

2 1/4 CUPS FLOUR

1/4 CUP MILK

1 PINCH SALT

PIE CRUST INSTRUCTIONS

Cut the butter in pieces and combine with flour in the bowl of a food processor. Pulse until crumbly. Add milk and salt and pulse until mixture just holds together—don't overmix. Refrigerate for 1 hour before use.

CRÈME CARAMEL

SERVES: 8

PREPARATION TIME: 30 minutes,

plus cooling time

INGREDIENTS

For the caramel sauce:

1 CUP WATER

2 CUPS SUGAR

2 TABLESPOONS LEMON JUICE

For the custard:

2 CUPS MILK

2 CUPS HALF-AND-HALF

8 FRESH EGGS

1 CUP SUGAR

2 TABLESPOONS VANILLA EXTRACT

WHIPPED CREAM TO SERVE

INSTRUCTIONS

Preheat the oven to 275°F. Make the caramel sauce: boil the water, sugar, and lemon juice in a heavy saucepan until the mixture turns a dark golden brown. Working quickly, cover the bottoms of 8 ramekins 3 inches high and 4 inches in diameter with the caramel sauce. Set the ramekins aside and prepare the custard. Heat the milk and half-and-half in a saucepan just until small bubbles form at the side of the pan. Remove from heat and set aside. Beat the eggs, sugar, and vanilla in a bowl and add the milk mixture gradually. Strain the mixture into a clean bowl, then pour into ramekins. Place the cups in a deep pan, fill the pan with water to 1/2 inch from the rims of the cups, and bake for about 1 hour until the custard feels firm and set. Remove from the oven and refrigerate overnight. To serve, use a thin paring knife to slice around the edges of the ramekins. Invert each on a plate, and serve with chilled whipped cream.

MARINADES

The secret to making a tenderizing marinade is to use at least one acidic ingredient that will break down the muscle fibers in the steak. For the best flavor, use fresh ingredients when possible, and add a little oil to the mixture so that the ingredients will stick to the surface of the steak while it is being charred. Typical acid ingredients include wine; vinegar; fresh papaya, pineapple, and figs; ginger; yogurt; lemon juice; soy sauce; and mustard. Mix them up according to your own taste. Each pound (450g) of meat will need about one-quarter cup (60ml) of marinade. Marinate a tender steak for no more than two hours. A tough cut of steak might demand twenty-four hours, but that is the outside limit. Too much time in the bath might make your steak mushy. And what would you rather taste—marinade or meat?

SAUCE

A little pan sauce can do wonders for a steak, especially if it is not as perfect a specimen as the dry-aged beauties served at Smith & Wollensky. There is no real trick to pan sauce. In fact, that is the trick—keeping it plain and simple and not ruining it with a lot of fancy ingredients. Panfry your steak, searing it well. Take the steak out of the pan. If there is a visible amount of fat in the pan, try to sponge or spoon some of it out. Then reheat the remaining drippings, add one-quarter cup (60ml) of beef broth or water (chicken broth will work, too), and the same amount of red or white wine, a pinch of salt and pepper, and bring it to a boil. Cook a few minutes until the liquid is reduced by half, and serve it with the sliced or whole steak.

CHEF'S BUTTER

There are those who say a good steak is ruined by gussying it up with spices, sauces, or marinades. But it is hard to fault a little pat of chef's butter melting on top of a good steak. It's a simple concept: butter flavored with garlic and chives. And it is easy to make. Slightly soften a stick of butter and cream in 1/2 teaspoon finely minced garlic and 1 teaspoon or so of fresh chives. Store the mixture in a custard cup or small bowl in the refrigerator. When it comes time to serve your steak, shave off a thin slice of the butter

and set it right atop the center of the meat, so that as it melts it glazes the surface and drips down the edges to blend with the natural juices. Here are some variations that are prepared in the same way as the classic:

MUSTARD BUTTER

1 stick (125g) butter

1 tbsp prepared mustard

1/2 tsp mustard powder

WATERCRESS BUTTER

1 stick (125g) butter

Leaves of one bunch of watercress, finely chopped

BLUE CHEESE BUTTER

1 stick (125g) butter

2 1/2 oz (70g) blue cheese, half of it chunked, half of it puréed

RED WINE BUTTER

1 stick (125g) butter

1 shallot, chopped

1 cup (250ml) red wine, simmered until reduced to 1 tbsp, and cooled

FRESH GREEN PEPPER BUTTER

1 stick (125g) butter

2 tbsp chopped green pepper

PAPRIKA BUTTER

1 stick (125g) butter

1 tbsp mild paprika

1/2 fresh or canned pimento, diced

LIVER-SAUSAGE BUTTER

1 stick (125g) butter

Dash of brandy

Dash of paté spice

2 1/2 oz (70g) liver-sausage

HORSERADISH BUTTER

1 stick (125g) butter

1 to 2 tsp jarred horseradish

AVOCADO BUTTER

1 stick (125g) butter

Meat of 1 ripe avocado, half of it diced, half of it puréed

Salt and pepper to taste

HERB BUTTER

1 stick (125g) butter

1/3 tsp each of chopped parsley, thyme, basil, fennel, and powdered ginger

1 tsp capers

1/2 garlic clove, peeled and minced

1 tsp mustard powder

BELOW: THE RAREST AND MOST SOUGHT-AFTER WINES SHOW THE PASSAGE OF TIME AS THEY WAIT IN THE WINE CELLAR FOR THE RIGHT MOMENT AND THE RIGHT CUSTOMER.

WINE

What goes with a steak besides a strong fork and a sharp knife? Red wine, of course—preferably a full-bodied variety. Remember, the wine is going to be competing with a perfect steak for your mouth's attentions. If the steak is grilled or broiled, it will have a more direct, unfussy flavor that goes well with a straightforward wine, such as an Opus One. Steak that has been transformed with sauces and other ingredients, as at a Thai restaurant, for example, must be matched with wine on a case-by-case basis, although red is always a good rule of thumb.

SUGGESTIONS

ROAST PRIME RIB

This tender cut is particularly well suited to a Pinot Noir. The light flavor of the beef is set off with the

BELOW: WHILE SOME CUTS ARE PARTICULARLY WELL SUITED TO CERTAIN TYPES OF WINE, THE BOTTOM LINE IS THAT ANY GOOD RED AND A GREAT STEAK MAKE FOR A WINNING COMBINATION.

finesse of the pinot grape, and not overpowered as it can be by the largesse of a Cabernet. Some suggestions:

- Corton, Bonneau du Martray 1985
- Nuits-St.-Georges, R. Arnoux 1993
- King Estate Pinot Noir, Oregon 1996
- Rex Hill Reserve Pinot Noir, Oregon 1994
- Robert Sinskey "Los Carneros," Napa 1996
- Panther Creek "Freedom Hill," Pinot Noir, Oregon 1996
- Pommard 1er Cru "les Rugiens" J. Marc Bouley 1996

FILET MIGNON

Once again, this is a "lighter" style of beef, so a Pinot Noir will work particularly well, as will some of the lighter style Merlots, Riojas, and Sangioveses.

- E. Costanti Brunello Di Montalcino, Italy 1995
- Chateau La Grave à Pomerol 1995
- Shafer "Firebreak" 1996
- Rioja San Vicente, Spain 1994
- Pinot Noir, Salitage, Australia 1994
- Seghesio Winery, Sangiovese 1996
- Badia a Coltibuono, Sangioveto, Italy 1994

SIRLOIN

The big, beefy flavor of the sirloin deserves a big, beefy wine. Cabernet Sauvignons, big-bodied Merlots, Bordeaux-style blends, and Rhone Valley Syrahs are all good bets.

- Yarra Yerring Dry Red Wine #1, Aust. 1992
- Penfolds Grange Hermitage, any year
- Chapoutier, Hermitage 1990
- Jordan Cabernet Sauvignon 1994
- Matanzas Creek Merlot 1996
- Robert Mondavi "Oakford Ranch" Cabernet 1995
- Quintessa "Rutherford" Napa 1995
- Château Gruaud Larose 1990
- Château Pichon Longueville, Comtesse de Lalande 1986
- Château Giscours 1995
- Duckhorn "Three Palms" Merlot 1996
- Shafer "Hillside Select" Cabernet 1994

RIB STEAK

Like the sirloin, the rib steak has a big taste that's best accompanied by a full-bodied wine like a Cabernet.

- Opus One 1987
- St. Francis "Old-vines" Zinfandel 1997
- Château Cheval Blanc 1990
- Caymus "Special Selection" 1994
- Château Haut-Brion 1990
- E & J Gallo Estate Cabernet Sauvignon 1995
- Stag's Leap "Cask 23" any year
- Summus, Banfi, Italy 1995
- Amarone "il Bosco" Cesari 1990
- Silver Oak, Napa or Alexander Valley any year
- Geyser Peak Shiraz, Sonoma 1995

KNIVES

———◆———

Smith & Wollensky patrons slice their steaks with high-quality, tempered steel knives, although that is pure overkill, because these steaks are so tender that you could cut them with a wooden butter spreader. But just in case you encounter a steak that requires good carving and slicing skills, here are some tips to help you along.

First, have a freshly sharpened eight- or ten-inch (20 or 25cm) slicing knife handy, along with a paring knife. Look at your steak and determine which way the grain, that is, the muscle fibers, is traveling. It is easiest for our teeth to get through a steak if the muscle fibers are cut short, rather than left in long strands. So slice your steak across the grain for the tenderest bites.

If you are serving steak that you slice before bringing to the table, let the steak sit, whole, for a few minutes after cooking to bathe itself in its own interior juices. Then slice it on a board with a built-in trough, or set the board on a platter that will catch the juices. If you are serving a bone-in steak, such as a porterhouse, cut the bone away before slicing the steak, then slice the meat across the grain. The steak will have better texture and taste if you cut generous slices, about half an inch (12mm) thick.

FINAL TIPS, SUGGESTIONS, AND REMINDERS

———◆———

The classic steak is cooked unadorned—without any seasoning except a little pepper and salt. But don't be afraid to be creative. Many people enjoy steak stir-fried, sautéed, cut in cubes for shish-kebabs, and even eaten in salads.

Here are some suggestions for making your steak taste its best:

◆ Cook it appropriately. Very tender steaks, such as filets mignons and sirloins, are good for broiling, grilling, and panfrying. If a steak is a little tougher, such as a flank steak, marinate it first before choosing one of these methods. Or you can braise a tough cut like a chuck steak in liquid to soften it up.

◆ Make sure the surface of your meat is dry before you cook it—the steak will brown better if it is dry.

OPPOSITE: STEAK WOLLENSKY, A SLICED SIRLOIN ACCOMPANIED BY FRIED ONION RINGS, IS A PERENNIAL CUSTOMER FAVORITE.

BELOW: STUFFED LOBSTER WITH CRAB AND SHRIMP IS SURE TO WHET THE APPETITES OF THOSE WHO JUST AREN'T IN THE MOOD FOR BEEF. (PERISH THE THOUGHT AND PASS THE STEAK KNIVES, PLEASE!) **OPPOSITE:** THE WOODEN BOOTHS IN THE NEW YORK DINING ROOM ARE RARELY EMPTY; THEY'RE USUALLY FILLED WITH PEOPLE FOR WHOM MAKING DEALS OVER A GOOD STEAK CONSTITUTES A SATISFYING MEAL.

Pat it with a towel if necessary.

◆ Leave a thin layer of fat when you trim the steaks. If you want a completely fat-free surface, trim any remaining fat after cooking. The fat improves the flavor.

◆ Be sure to cook the steak at a temperature that allows the inside to warm up before the outside is charred.

◆ Turn your steaks with tongs only. According to true steak fanatics, a fork will cause the juices to flow out, draining the steak of precious flavor.

◆ These same fanatics may tell you to never, ever put salt on a steak before you cook it. They say the salt will draw out the juices. Others disagree, saying the salt won't have this effect in such a short time. They believe that the salt helps the steak brown, and makes it taste a lot better. Clearly, this is a personal decision.

◆ Try using a rub. Mix your favorite dried herbs and spices in a bowl. Use this mix dry, or add oil, garlic, or mustard to make a wet rub. Before cooking the steak, rub this mixture into the surface of the meat. It won't tenderize the meat like a marinade, but it will add a lot of flavor.

◆ Steaks taste better if you let them sit for a couple of minutes after cooking them, to distribute the juices more uniformly throughout the meat.

◆ And the final tip: cook a little more meat than you will eat, so you can look forward to a nice steak sandwich.

SMITH & WOLLENSKY AROUND THE NATION

NEW YORK

797 THIRD AVENUE AT 49TH ST.

(212) 753-1530

The original, since 1977. Smith & Wollensky's flagship restaurant is the best-known steakhouse in the world—the one the New York Times called "a steakhouse to end all arguments." With its casually elegant interior of brass and polished wood, a 50,000-bottle wine cellar—and, of course, the world's finest aged beef—this award-winning restaurant set the standard for New York City steakhouses, and for the Smith & Wollenskys to follow.

MIAMI BEACH

1 WASHINGTON AVE. AT SOUTH POINTE PARK

(305) 673-2800

Located on the water in Miami's fashionable South Beach section, this 600-seat restaurant offers unparalleled views of both the Atlantic Ocean and the downtown skyline through its huge picture windows. Befitting the balmy climate of South Florida, the restaurant features an outdoor cafe where guests can dine al fresco, as well as a cigar bar, the casual Wollensky's Grill, and several private dining areas.

CHICAGO

318 NORTH STATE ST. AT MARINA CITY

(312) 670-9900

When it opened in April 1998, Smith & Wollensky's Chicago restaurant made a city that takes its steak seriously sit up and take notice. Located next to the landmark Marina City towers in the River North area, the restaurant has intimate dining areas spread over two floors, with large windows offering panoramic views of the Chicago River. Private dining areas include a 130-seat room with wraparound windows, a Cigar Room, and a Wine Room for small parties.

NEW ORLEANS

1009 POYDRAS ST. AT S. RAMPART

(504) 561-0770

Opened in October 1998, Smith & Wollensky's Big Easy outpost occupies a landmark 19th-century building that was formerly home to Maylie's, a classic French Creole restaurant that opened on Poydras Street in 1876. Located two blocks from the Superdome and an easy walk from New Orleans' French Quarter, the restaurant has 400 seats on two levels, and features an outdoor patio, a private party room, and a 15,000-bottle wine cellar.

LAS VEGAS

3767 LAS VEGAS BLVD., BETWEEN TROPICANA AND HARMON

(702) 862-4100

Smith & Wollensky brings the relaxed elegance of a New York City steakhouse to the heart of Glitter Gulch. The 600-seat restaurant boasts the familiar decor, a cigar bar, private dining areas, a peerless wine cellar, and a 12-seat, glass-enclosed "Kitchen Table."

WASHINGTON, D.C.

1112 NINETEENTH ST. NW, BETWEEN L AND M

(202) 466-1100

Situated on Washington's "Restaurant Row," this Smith & Wollensky features indoor seating for more than 300, plus a sidewalk cafe. Several private dining rooms and a climate-controlled, glass-enclosed "Kitchen Table" offer space for special occasions.

MIAMI BEACH

CHICAGO

LAS VEGAS

NEW ORLEANS

GLOSSARY OF COMMON STEAK TERMINOLOGY

AGING: A process used to make beef taste better. Fresh beef can be wet-aged in vacuum packages, along with its juices, or dry-aged for several weeks in a well-ventilated walk-in cooler. Aging releases amino acids that break down the muscle fibers of the steak, tenderizing it and giving it a heightened flavor.

BLOOM: A color change from deep purple to pinkish-red due to oxidation when vacuum-packed beef is opened.

CONNECTIVE TISSUE: The tissue in beef that holds the meat to the bone, and binds the muscles together.

DRY-AGING: The method used by Smith & Wollensky for curing steaks by storing them, uncovered, in a well-ventilated and cooled locker. The constant flow of fresh air over the meat allows it to age slowly, developing a darker patina, greater tenderness, and richer flavor.

FREEZER BURN: Dehydration and oxidation of frozen meat due to inadequate wrapping. Signs of freezer burn include dark brown or grayish color of thawed meat.

HEME IRON: The type of iron most easily absorbed by the human body, found in beef, but not in vegetables and grains.

INSPECTION: A service to the public by the U.S. Department of Agriculture. Inspections of beef are intended to assure consumers that the meat they buy is safe, and has been carefully handled during processing.

MARBLING: Intramuscular fat that collects between the red muscle fibers of beef. Generally, the more marbling, the juicier the steak and the better the flavor.

MIDDLE MEATS: The rib and loin cuts of beef, including many of the most popular steaks.

MYOGLOBIN: A protein responsible for the color of meat, because it binds oxygen in the cells. When myoglobin is exposed to oxygen in the air, it turns into a protein called oxymyoglobin, which makes the meat turn red.

QUALITY GRADES: Quality rating of beef by the U.S. Department of Agriculture. Inspectors determine the grade based on the amount of marbling in the meat, the age of the animal at slaughter, and the color of the meat, among other factors. The top grade is Prime, followed in descending order of quality by Choice, Select, Standard, Commerical, Utility, Cutter, and Canner.

URMIS: An acronym for Uniform Retail Meat Identity Standards. URMIS is a uniform system for labeling meat sold in the United States, so that identically labeled cuts of meat are the same anatomical cut throughout the country.

WHOLESALE and PRIMAL CUTS: Portions of carcasses and sides of beef that can be trimmed further into steaks by butchers. These cuts include the rib, short loin, and sirloin.

WET- or VACUUM-AGING: The process of aging meat in air-free vacuum packaging. Currently the most common way to age steaks.

YIELD GRADING: A method for estimating how many steaks can be obtained from a certain portion of meat.

STEAK TO GO

Now you can enjoy Smith & Wollensky's delicious steaks at home. The same dry-aged prime beef offered in the restaurant, along with the famous oversized Smith & Wollensky steak knives, can be ordered toll-free and shipped anywhere in the country. In addition, fresh steak, steak sauce, knives, and cigars may be purchased on-site at any Smith & Wollensky location. For "Steak To Go," just dial 1-877-783-2555.

INDEX